The Retirement Flight Plan

ARRIVING SAFELY AT FINANCIAL SUCCESS

John T. Hagensen,
MSFS, CFS®, CAS®, CTS®, CES®, CIS®

Outspoken Fiduciary LLC

John T. Hagensen/Outspoken Fiduciary LLC
info@keystonewealthpartners.com
https://keystonewealthpartners.com

Book layout ©2015 BookDesignTemplates.com

The Retirement Flight Plan/ John T. Hagensen. —1st ed.
ISBN 978-0-578-58744-8

Contents

To my six children: Bek, Sha, Cruz, Zaya, Jude, and Aria.
May God grant you the wisdom to know what is right,
and the courage to do it.

If you fail to plan, you are planning to fail.

—BENJAMIN FRANKLIN

Preface

O n July 21 and 22, 1999, most of Manhattan's Upper East Side was shut down. Officials closed 88th through 91st Streets to traffic along the three blocks spanning Lexington Avenue to Fifth Avenue. On July 23, mourners— donned in black, faces covered—flocked to the area, convening at the 126-year-old church of St. Thomas More. Only 350 people were invited to attend the service, but around the country, a collective tear was shed that day.[1]

The memorial service followed a five-day Coast Guard search-and-rescue mission off the coast of Martha's Vineyard in Massachusetts. The Coast Guard does not usually conduct such long search efforts. Search procedure stipulates the mission desist when there is no chance of a missing person's survival. That length of time varies. It depends mostly on the ocean's temperature. In the 52°F New England Atlantic, a missing person would succumb within a few hours. A five-day search was unprecedented. It was criticized by some as an excessive effort, especially for three private citizens.

President Bill Clinton made the executive decision to prolong the recovery mission, however. In the face of scrutiny, he said, "if

---

[1] CNN. July 23, 1999. "Mourners Arrive for N.Y. Mass."
http://www.cnn.com/US/9907/23/kennedy.plane.03/index.html

anyone believes that [my decision] was wrong, the Coast Guard is not at fault—I am." He couldn't allow the search to end before accomplishing its mission. "It was the right thing to do."[2]

After all, you can't give up when the primary target of your search is America's favorite son—John F. Kennedy Jr.

July 16 had been a dreary Friday along the New England coast. The Kennedy family hoped the weather would improve before cousin Rory's wedding on Saturday. John Jr. had a regular day: he met with the editors for his magazine, *George*, worked out at his local gym, and then set about packing for the weekend's festivities. At some point, John called another pilot, Kyle Bailey, and asked him to prepare Kennedy's plane for that evening's flight.

Traffic was heavy in the city, so "John-John" was late arriving at Essex County Airport in Caldwell, New Jersey. His passengers, wife Carolyn Kennedy and sister-in-law Lauren Bessette, arrived separately, and also late. Most of the maintenance workers at the airport had already gone home. Kennedy was surprised to find Kyle Bailey still at the airport, though. Earlier, Bailey had told John of his own plans to fly to Martha's Vineyard that evening. Although Bailey was a more experienced pilot, he explained he'd adjusted his plans in the face of the storm that loomed over the New England coast. Little did the Kennedy family realize how fatal that interchange would prove.[3]

It was 8:39 p.m. when JFK Jr. and his family took off in his Piper PA-32 Saratoga II. The weather was nasty and worsening. Conditions over Martha's Vineyard were reported as hazy with only six miles of visibility. Kennedy did not hold a full pilot's

[2] Mike Allen. *The New York Times.* July 22, 1999. "Bodies from Kennedy Crash are Found."
https://www.nytimes.com/1999/07/22/us/bodies-from-kennedy-crash-are-found.html
[3] *The Guardian.* July 25, 1999. "Why John Kennedy Crashed."
https://www.theguardian.com/world/1999/jul/25/kennedy.usa

license. Instead, he had an intermediary certificate. It permitted him to fly only when visibility was better than five miles.

Kyle Bailey watched the small single-engine plane take off. That evening, he told his family, "I can't believe he's going up in this weather."[4]

About an hour into the flight, Martha's Vineyard should have been within sight. Instead, there was a haze of nothingness. Humidity rising from the sea left a thick, fog-like wall in the warm summer sky. JFK Jr. was staring at a sheet of darkness: no horizon, no lights, no orientation whatsoever.

Soon, emotion got the better of him. His mind started playing tricks. He lost his bearings and lost control of the aircraft. Just a few miles short of their destination, the Kennedys crashed into the frigid sea at 5,000 feet per minute, about fifty-seven miles per hour. They descended in what pilots call a "graveyard spiral"— corkscrewing uncontrollably.[5]

Retirement Weather Status

Today's retirement conditions, much like the conditions on the fateful night of John F. Kennedy Jr.'s death, can be unpredictable. For some, everything falls nicely into place, and retirement goes off without a hitch—at least for a time. But, after a lifetime of hard work, you can't afford to go into retirement just hoping that everything works out. You must plan for the worst.

What's especially tragic about JFK Jr.'s accident is it was totally preventable. Flying conditions were less than ideal, yes. But a

---

[4] Ibid.

[5] Mike Allen. *The New York Times.* July 22, 1999. "Bodies from Kennedy Crash are Found."
https://www.nytimes.com/1999/07/22/us/bodies-from-kennedy-crash-are-found.html

more capable pilot could have completed the journey without much trouble.

Before transitioning to the financial industry, I was a commercial airline pilot flying out of Los Angeles International Airport. I can tell you, low visibility is just a part of the game. Kennedy's downfall was partly attributable to a mixture of inexperience and overconfidence.

For one thing, John Jr. elected to fly without a qualified co-pilot. Before the flight, one of Kennedy's instructors offered to accompany the family, but John turned him down. That decision was surprising, because JFK Jr. had often enlisted the support of a more experienced pilot in the past, even for much simpler flights. Had a certified instructor been present, the group would probably have arrived at their destination.

Kennedy also neglected to use the tools at his disposal. His airplane, the Piper Saratoga, was equipped with an excellent autopilot and John knew how to use it. Yet, when the search team recovered the aircraft, they discovered that autopilot had not been engaged at the time of the plane's crash. Textbook overconfidence from an inexperienced pilot.[6]

Inexperience and overconfidence are traits many of us possess, and they may plague many a soon-to-be retiree. After all, it's one thing to earn money, but it's another to save enough to create sustainable income for thirty non-working years. It's easy to think everything is under control when circumstances are favorable. JFK Jr. had flown many times when the weather was good for flying. He misgauged his ability and assumed he had the skillset to navigate more treacherous weather. It cost him his life. Some have

---

[6] *AOPA.* July 5, 2010. "10 Mistakes JFK Jr. Made: Lessons from a National Tragedy." https://www.aopa.org/news-and-media/all-news/2010/july/pilot/10-mistakes-jfk-jr-made

found they are similarly unprepared when the financial climate turns for the worst.

My father-in-law has been a financial professional for more than thirty years. Now he is an adviser with the firm I founded, Keystone Wealth Partners. He's seen how dynamic and volatile the economy can be. I remember him telling me a story of a couple who came into his office in January 2009. Just a few days earlier, the Case-Shiller Home Price Index had reported the largest drop in home prices in recorded history. Before that, in September 2008, the Dow Jones Industrial Average (Dow-Jones) tanked. In just one day, it plummeted 777 points. Never had the market dried up so quickly. It was devastating. For anyone hoping to retire, it was like flying into an ominous wall of haze.

The couple who visited my father-in-law was distraught. The wife couldn't hold back her tears. She was sixty-two and her husband was sixty-four. Before the crash, they were two years from retiring. Now, it looked like that would be impossible.

"We've run a small farm and agriculture supply business for almost forty years," she said, looking at her husband for support. "It often involves physically demanding work. We can't keep doing it much longer."

After examining their finances, my father-in-law was reluctant to tell them that, based on their losses, it would probably be another five to seven years before they would recover enough of their assets to think about retirement. They had lost almost 40 percent of their nest egg in the stock market crash.

"But our stockbroker told us that our portfolio was diversified," said the wife mournfully. "We thought our money was safe. This wasn't supposed to happen. Why didn't anyone warn us this was coming?"

My father-in-law didn't tell them, but the question was naïve. *No one* saw the market crash of 2008 coming. If it had been so easily foreseeable, it would never have happened! Regardless of what some stockbrokers might say, it is impossible to time the stock market perfectly. Sure, there are a lot of graphs and charts and software that make predictions about the future. But that's the best they can do—make *predictions*. Nothing is set in stone. Only hindsight is 20/20. Looking back now, it's obvious what went wrong. The housing market was barreling toward a disaster. Mortgages were approved left and right with little in the way of eligibility verification. A "housing bubble" developed, and then it popped. Big investment banks like Lehman Brothers closed their doors and the stock market couldn't withstand the hit. Many who blindly trusted in the stock market faced severe financial setbacks.

The "Wall Street guys" would have you believe a capable stockbroker and a "diversified portfolio" are the keys to financial success. For a certain demographic, that might be true. Not soon-to-be retirees, though. Responsible retirement planning protects your money from stock market volatility and ensures that your retirement income will be there when you need it—especially when bad weather looms on the horizon.

How Do You Picture Retirement?

What's your idea of retirement? That's one of my favorite questions for new clients. The answers I get are never disappointing, and they're almost never the same.

"Golf. I just want to play golf," said one man. "If I could spend every day of thirty years out on a green, I'd be a happy man."

One couple had more ambitious plans. "We've led a pretty mundane life," said the wife, "but we've always wanted to be a little more adventurous. We just never had the time. I think we'll have to try sky-diving at some point. Maybe bungee jumping, too. Retirement is not going to be our time to slow down!"

Another couple wanted to travel. "Paris, London, Rome—we'll hit those first," the husband said. His wife continued, "But then we'd like to visit some places off the beaten path. Madagascar looks gorgeous, and New Zealand, too."

Some have more traditional ideas of retirement. One couple had raised six children. They had nine grandchildren and counting. They had a beautiful Arizona ranch where they hoped to watch their grandkids grow up over the many years to come. With a half-dozen children of my own, I especially appreciated their retirement agenda.

Regardless of how you plan to spend your retirement years, there is one absolute constant: you need the funds to support it. That may sound bleak, but it doesn't have to be. JFK Jr. didn't survive that harrowing night, but *he could have*. The conditions weren't impossible; he was just ill-prepared. The same is true of our financial journey. You *can* live out your dream retirement!

In this book, we will cover several financial strategies. Some of the ideas may be new to you. You won't find a mainstream financial mantra designed to push a product. Instead, you'll learn about financial principles that work. Please, approach the information with an open mind. You may be surprised to discover that ideas you thought were basic no longer apply to today's financial landscape or your personal situation. That's not an unusual conclusion.

Embrace the change. After all, if something you thought was true was actually false, when would you want to find out? When there's still time to adjust, or when it's too late and an outdated idea may have jeopardized your financial future?

Remember the days before smartphones when everyone drove around with a GPS suction-cupped to the front windshield? It was the height of technology at the time. These days, those GPS devices are almost nonexistent. Embarking on the journey to retirement with old-fashioned ideas is like using a clunky old GPS to find your way through a newly developed area. Sure, some things may not have changed, but ultimately, you're going to get lost.

My objective with this book is to educate and inform. You'll find the truth about money, investments, wealth preservation, taxes, and more. The book will allow you to make informed decisions when it comes to your retirement. What you'll find here is more than just my opinion. It is the product of decades of research from many of the brightest minds in finance. Finance can be an overwhelming subject, but it needn't be. With a little forethought and planning, you can fly confidently into retirement. So, turn the page and let's get started. Be assured, you can arrive safely at your destination: financial success!

Section One:

Your Flight to Retirement

If you don't know where you are going,
you'll end up someplace else.

—YOGI BERRA

CHAPTER ONE

The Twenty-First Century Passenger

If you drive about half an hour northwest of Chandler, Arizona, where our flagship office is, you'll arrive in Phoenix. The state capital is a bustling city, ripe with industry and culture. Locals and visitors alike enjoy performances at several theaters, the opera, the symphony, and the ballet. Four universities infuse the "Valley of the Sun" with a youthful and trendy presence. That's not to say history is neglected. On the contrary, Phoenix's rich heritage is commemorated in museums scattered about the metropolitan area, especially emphasizing Native American art and culture. Phoenix also is the place to be for sports lovers.

Phoenix is home to four professional sports franchises, including the Arizona Diamondbacks of Major League Baseball. The D-backs were formed as an expansion team in 1998. The same year, a new stadium was built for them in downtown Phoenix, called Chase Field (if you've been a fan long enough, you may remember it as Bank One Ballpark). The stadium is something of a wonder. The field is natural grass, the traditional choice for ballparks. Most natural grass playing fields are in open air stadiums to provide the grass with life-sustaining sunlight. Chase Field, however, has a retractable roof—one of the first of its kind. The design took some ingenuity and added expense, but it was worth it. It was almost mandatory, in fact, when you consider Phoenix's extreme climate.

At the height of baseball season, the average temperature in Phoenix sits at about 100 degrees Fahrenheit. It's not uncommon for highs to reach well into three digits, exceeding 110 degrees. Without its retractable roof, Chase Field would be a veritable hotbox. Still, the ballpark often gets stuffy, especially at peak season when the stadium is full. If you've ever been to a game on a blazing summer day, you know what I mean.

Imagine a hot day at the ballpark, the stadium packed to capacity. That's just shy of 50,000 people. That number may seem arbitrary, and you may be wondering what this has to do with retirement, but there is a point: that is roughly the number of people who retire in the United States every five days. Can you picture yourself at Chase Field? The sun beating down, the smell of hotdogs and peanuts wafting overhead, children laughing, and D-back baseball caps as far as the eye can see. Now imagine all those people retiring in less than a week's time.

It's even more impressive to think these droves of retirees will continue to vacate the workforce for the next ten-plus years. Ten thousand people a day are reaching retirement. History has never seen the likes. It makes sense, though, because today's retiree is a product of the baby boom.

The Baby Boomer Generation

The twentieth century set off with a bang in America. It seemed to many that humankind had reached the pinnacle of civility and refinement. Technology was largely to thank. American journalist Hebert Kaufman spoke for the nation when he said in 1913,

THE RETIREMENT FLIGHT PLAN | 3

"'Impossibility' is now an old-fashioned word . . . Almost every dream of the past is a reality today." Among those dreams was an end to war. Then 1914 rolled around, and a darkness seemed to settle over the world scene.

World War I left the American psyche in tatters. The optimism that had carried the world into a new century was all but gone. If any positivity remained after World War I, the Great Depression and World War II dealt it a fatal blow.

Then came the 1950s. Although fifty years late, it was finally the twentieth century of which America had dreamed. Some wars still brewed, but the threat of global conflict was fading into the past. For decades, the American people had forfeited normal lives to protect the greater good. There'd been little time to develop a career or raise a family. By the time World War II ended in 1945, Americans had a lot of catching up to do.

The United States economy was booming. The technology boom of the early 1900s had focused on weaponry. Now it was repurposed to improve the everyday lives of the American people. Former luxuries were becoming mainstream; technology had never been more accessible.

Whenever times are good, people make babies. Well, things were *really* good in the late 1940s and 1950s. For the better part of thirty years, American men had been spending their prime years at battle across the sea. At last, they were home and they weren't about to waste any time. In 1946, 3.4 million babies were born in the United States. That marked a 20 percent jump in live births from the previous year. In fact, October of 1946 included most of the births for that entire year. That's exactly nine months after World War II ended, by the way.

Thus began the "baby boom." The number of babies born per year would continue to climb over the next twenty-eight years until the baby boomer generation was officially cut off in 1964.

Over that three-decade span, the birth rate exceeded four million babies per year *every year*. By comparison, annual births in the United States have only exceeded four million thirteen times since 1990, and not since 2009.[7]

By 1964, the United States population swelled to an all-time high. The young baby boomers represented 40 percent of the entire country. They would be special for more than just their sheer volume, though. Baby boomers would come to have a greater socio-economic effect on the United States—and the world—than any generation before them.[8]

Who's Really the *Greatest* Generation?

Baby boomers' parents fancied themselves "the Greatest Generation." The term wasn't popularized until 1998 when legendary journalist Tom Brokaw published a book with the same name. The attribution is not farfetched. Brokaw describes in his book an unbreakable generation that triumphed over Great Depression deprivation and Nazi fascism. The G.I. Generation, as they're officially known (with some overlap from the Silent Generation), was great indeed. Still, baby boomers have a strong case for being the greatest generation America has ever seen.

Baby boomers were born into more favorable circumstances than their parents. But they adopted the same powerful work ethic that drove their parents to greatness. Baby boomers made the most of the immense opportunity that lay before them. They went on to make a greater contribution to American society than any generation before. Even if we adjust for inflation, baby boomers

---

[7] *Statista*. 2019. "Number of Births in the United States from 1990 to 2017 (In Millions)." https://www.statista.com/statistics/195908/number-of-births-in-the-united-states-since-1990/

[8] History.com. "Baby Boomers." https://www.history.com/topics/world-war-ii/baby-boomers-video

are still the highest-earning generation in American history.[9] Moreover, this generation drove industry to new heights, revolutionized technology, broke down social barriers, and introduced civil liberties. This is the generation that tore down Jim Crow laws, overturned communism, and put a man on the moon. These Americans invented the internet, for goodness' sake!

Now, baby boomers are preparing to turn in their briefcases for golf bags. Can you believe it? If you think their exodus from the workforce would dramatically affect the world, you'd be right. Is this contender for "greatest generation" prepared to retire?

For the most part, no.

Baby boomers first started to retire in 2011. The Associated Press conducted a survey to estimate how well boomers had readied themselves for this new chapter in their lives. The results indicated that most baby boomers weren't ready *at all*.

One question prompted baby boomers to rate how confident they were in their financial preparedness. Were they confident they could live comfortably in retirement? Of respondents, 67 percent said they were confident. And about 59 percent think they will be able to pay for medical expenses, with 52 percent saying they believe they will be able to afford long-term care. Although this is a good chunk of retirees who are confident in their finances, that doesn't necessarily mean these people are actually *able* to provide for themselves in retirement. And what about the other 48 percent of retirees who are not confident in their ability to pay for long-term care? Or the 33 percent who don't think they could afford retirement at all?[10]

---

[9] Meredith Turits. BBC. December 6, 2018. "Are Millennials on Track to Become the Richest Generation?"
http://www.bbc.com/capital/story/20181205-with-boomers-wealth-to-inherit-will-millennials-get-rich
[10] Employee Benefit Research Institute, Greenwald & Associates. April 23, 2019. "2019 Retirement Confidence Survey Summary Report."

Unfortunately, some other statistics explain many retirees' apprehensions about retiring comfortably. In 2018, Forbes published an article on baby boomer retirement. Many of the statistics were alarming, but perhaps none were more frightening than this: 42 percent of baby boomers have nothing saved for retirement. *Nothing.* Not even a bit stored away in a 401(k).[11]

Baby boomers are excellent earners. There is no denying that. They're hard workers, and many earn substantial incomes. The problem is, generally speaking, baby boomers are much better at spending their money than saving it.

Their parents knew what it was like to be penniless. Boomers, on the other hand, have enjoyed much better circumstances. They grew up in America's golden era—a consumer's paradise. The credit card was on the rise, spending was easy, and saving was a nonstarter. Only now, that "spend first, save later" attitude is finally catching up.

A Longevity Crisis

People are living longer these days. It's a big problem. Okay, so that's not really a *problem.* Because who wouldn't want to live longer? Let me explain.

A rising standard of living in the United States has resulted in longer lives than ever before. Vanguard, an organization that specializes in investments and retirement, recently published an article called "Plan for a Long Retirement" that explained just how old you might live to be. According to its article, a sixty-five-year-old man has a 41 percent chance of reaching age eighty-five, as

https://www.ebri.org/docs/default-source/rcs/2019-rcs/2019-rcs-short-report.pdf?sfvrsn=85543f2f_4

[11] John Schneider and David Auten. *Forbes.* May 20, 2018. "5 Surprising Facts about Boomer Retirement."
https://www.forbes.com/sites/debtfreeguys/2018/05/20/5-surprising-facts-about-boomer-retirement/#44369ebd4562

well as a 20 percent chance of reaching age ninety. For women, it might be better to plan even *longer*. If you are a woman aged sixty-five today, you have a 53 percent chance of living to age eighty-five, as well as a 32 percent chance of living to age ninety.[12]

Do you know the fastest-growing age group in the United States? I'll give you a clue: It's not working-age people, and it's definitely not children (people are having fewer kids than ever). It's not even recent retirees. It's the eighty-five and older demographic. Some research estimates that within the next thirty years, the eighty-five-plus community will constitute as great a percentage of the nation's total population as did the entire cohort of Americans sixty-five and older in 1930. There is no doubt: we're living longer than our parents and their parents before them, and it's great.[13]

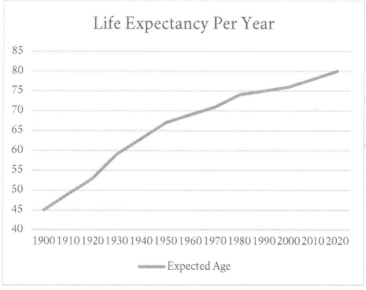

[12] Vanguard. 2019. "Plan for a Long Retirement." https://personal.vanguard.com/us/insights/retirement/plan-for-a-long-retirement-tool?lang=en

[13] *The Accounting Degree Review*. 2019. "The Crisis in Pensions and Retirement Plans." https://www.accounting-degree.org/retirement/

So why do I say that longer lives are a problem? Because living longer means retirement savings need to last longer, too, and that's proving to be a challenge for many.

Outliving one's money is a real concern for many retirees. In fact, it's their greatest fear. It supersedes fear of spiders, snakes, heights, being buried alive—you name it. Many would rather die than live to see their money run out.

In a survey conducted by the American Institute of CPAs (Certified Public Accountants) there was quite a strong conclusion. Financial planners were asked to identify one thing that concerned their clients more than anything else. Just under 60 percent responded that "running out of money was the top retirement concern for their clients." Clearly, something about the way people plan for retirement needs to change before these fears are realized.[14]

Why is Money Running Out?

Today's retirees face a major problem: today's standard retirement process was not designed for them.

In 1935, President Franklin D. Roosevelt enacted his New Deal program. It was created to nurse a crippled economy. Part of the New Deal was the Social Security Act. It established sixty-five as the magic number for retirement. At sixty-five, Americans qualified to collect a monthly check from the federal government. But remember all those statistics about life expectancy? In 1935, your chances of collecting much in the way of retirement income were bleak. At the time, a man's life expectancy barely surpassed fifty-nine. Women may have been fortunate enough to reach sixty-three. Either way, the average American wouldn't even live

---

[14] World Bank Group. 2019. "Life Expectancy at Birth, Total (Years)."
https://data.worldbank.org/indicator/SP.DYN.LE00.IN?locations=US

long enough to collect his or her Social Security check. That made it a lot easier for the program to fund the retired population.[15]

We've already established that today's retirement climate doesn't fit the 1935 mold. And yet, some expect government programs to continue making up for deficits in citizens' personal savings and investment returns.

Beside the challenge of more people looking to collect on Social Security, fewer are working to fund it. In 1950, assuming you made it to sixty-five and could retire, your Social Security check would have about sixteen American workers funding it with their taxes. Soon, however, nearly 30 percent of adults in the United States will not be working as the retired population continues to saturate. Already, in 2010 there were only 3.3 workers per Social Security beneficiary. It's predicted that by 2025, the ratio will drop to two workers per retiree. That number is strictly theoretical, however. It's unsustainable. To make up for the deficit, the federal government would have to expend 92 percent of all federal revenue for every retiree to receive his or her due payment. That's not going to happen.[16]

With the way things are now, it looks like Social Security will face a funding crisis in the next few decades—and soon-to-be retirees know it. 60 percent of them indicate they fear Social Security will have dried up by the time they are old enough to qualify. Of those already retired, 56 percent say they expect to have their benefits cut before they die. There is still time for corrective measures to improve things, but on its current route, Social Security is barreling toward disaster. To continue

---

[15] Robert Laura. *Forbes*. February 15, 2019. "Social Security Retirement Age Should Be 80."
https://www.forbes.com/sites/robertlaura/2019/02/15/social-security-retirement-age-should-be-80/#3663ce4e41c1
[16] ChildStats.gov. 2014. "POP2 Children..."
https://www.childstats.gov/americaschildren/tables/pop2.asp

supporting retirees over the next seventy-five years, Social Security would need to exceed funding by 46 trillion dollars.[17]

Just to be clear, that was not a typo. That's 46, not 4.6, and it's *trillion* with a big ol' T!

We're used to hearing the word trillion by now. News anchors and journalists throw it around casually. But what does it really mean? It's just the next step after billion and million. Just another three zeroes, right? How much bigger is it, really?

Allow me to illustrate. The difference between a billion and a trillion dollars is obscure to the average person. We know one is much bigger, but both figures are far beyond our reach. Instead, let's apply the numbers to a scale besides money: distance.

Picture a millimeter. That's about the width of a falling rain drop. It's basically inconsequential. One million millimeters, however, is a kilometer. Multiplying the measly millimeter by a million has increased its size, but a kilometer is still relatively short. An average person can walk that in about ten minutes. Depending on where you are in the town where the Keystone office is, Chandler, Arizona, the furthest you'll get is the adjacent town, Gilbert, where I live. A billion millimeters, however, is a formidable distance—1,000 kilometers, or 600 miles. From my office in Chandler, 1,000 kilometers will take you to Fresno, California, a ten-hour drive. If you were crazy enough to walk, it would take eight days without stopping.

One trillion millimeters, though . . . That's long enough to fly around the earth twenty-five times, or from one end of the sun to the other.

Here's another way to think about it, in case you're still not impressed by a trillion. A trillion dollars is such a large sum that there does not exist a single trillionaire in the world. (Although,

---

[17] *The Accounting Degree Review.* 2019. "The Crisis in Pensions and Retirement Plans." https://www.accounting-degree.org/retirement/

some sources predict that Amazon founder Jeff Bezos could become the first person to hit that landmark.[18]) There are several billionaires, though. One of the most famous is Microsoft founder, Bill Gates. He was, for a time, the richest man in the world. For simplicity, let's say that his net worth is an even 100 billion dollars. And, for the sake of illustration, let's pretend you make $100,000 a year. If you have $100,000, someone with a million dollars makes ten times more money than you. In effect, everything costs ten times less to that person, proportionally, than it does to you. So, a brand-new laptop costs the millionaire only $150. That shiny new Porsche? Maybe $7,000. A five-bedroom house? $50,000. It's kind of upsetting, right? Well, now imagine a billionaire.

To Bill Gates, a laptop costs—proportionally—just a few pennies, a Porsche costs less than a dollar, and a house may cost a few hundred dollars. Everything you could ever need in life would cost about $1,000.

I hope you've haven't chucked this book at the wall in disgust. I haven't even gotten to a trillionaire yet. To the hypothetical trillionaire, every necessity and pleasure in life could be bought for *one dollar.*

Now you can throw this book at the wall.

Does the magnitude of a *trillion* mean a little more to you now? With that in mind, think back to some of the reports you've heard on the news. For example, the government's trillions of dollars in debt, the trillions required to keep Social Security viable, or the trillions of dollars lost in 2000 and 2008 when the stock market crashed. Many lost almost half of their life savings in the financial crises that would punctuate the Great Recession. Their life plans

---

[18] Emmie Martin. CNBC Make It. July 27, 2017. "Jeff Bezos is Now the Riches Man in the World—and He Could also Become the First Trillionaire."
https://www.cnbc.com/2017/07/27/richest-man-alive-jeff-bezos-could-become-the-first-trillionaire.html

had shattered overnight. Some estimate people approaching retirement lost $2.8 trillion dollars in 2008. What's especially tragic to me is, much of that loss could have been avoided.

The twenty-first century retiree must contend with different circumstances than generations past. The journey to a successful retirement has changed and passengers must adjust. Government programs that have supported retirees for decades are not as reliable these days, and longevity is a double-edged sword. It's important that anyone approaching retirement recognize the game has changed. You can't play by the same old-fashioned rules. Ultimately, you cannot rely on anyone but yourself to fund your retirement. But where are modern day retirees headed, and how can they arrive at their destination safely? We'll examine the answer to that question in the next chapter.

CHAPTER TWO

Defining the Destination

Deep in the Himalayas, far from the hustle and bustle of modern civilization, lies the Mahalangur Himal mountain range. At its heart—straddling the border of Nepal and Tibet—is a mountain of extraordinary size. Over the centuries, the native people have given it various names: Kangchenjunga, Dhaulagiri, Deodungha, Chomolungma. You may know it better as Mount Everest.

Ever since surveyors discovered in 1856 that Mount Everest was the tallest mountain in the world (as measured from sea level; some other mountains are technically "taller"), the mountain has attracted the most extreme among adventurers and mountaineers. The first successful summit climb was achieved in 1953 by a New Zealander, Edmund Hillary, and a local Nepali Sherpa named Tenzing Norgay. However, dozens of attempts were made in previous decades.

As early as 1885, alpine climbers hypothesized that an ascent up Everest's treacherous flank was conceivable. In 1921, George Mallory led a reconnaissance mission to evaluate Everest's challenges and to begin plotting a route to the top. He returned in

1922 but failed to reach the summit. Finally, in 1924, Mallory set out on a third attempt more determined than ever. He wrote before his departure, "It is almost unthinkable that I shan't get to the top; I can't see myself coming down defeated." As fate would have it, Mallory never came down at all. He was last seen on June 8, 1934, fading into the distance. His body was recovered in 1999. Some believe he made it to the summit before succumbing to the cold and altitude. You can decide for yourself whether he was "defeated" or not.[19]

Mallory's death was a fitting prelude to subsequent failures over the next century. The mountain has become a wintry graveyard. Nearly 300 people have died attempting the perilous climb. In most cases, the extreme conditions make it too risky to retrieve the deceased climbers. The Nepalese government estimates that more than 200 bodies lie strewn across the mountainside—icy carcasses cocooned in the frozen landscape.

Adventurers die for several reasons. Exposure is the number one killer. Temperatures near the peak can get as low as -70 degrees Fahrenheit, and almost never exceed 0 degrees Fahrenheit. Hypothermia and severe frostbite are common. The extreme altitude above 8,000 meters is nicknamed the "death zone." Dwindling oxygen levels cause headaches, nausea and exhaustion—at the least. High altitude can also induce cerebral and pulmonary edema, which inhibit muscle control, impair speech, and give one hallucinations and severe coughing spells.

If exposure doesn't get you, then sudden storms, falls, and avalanches might do the trick. All in all, climbing Mount Everest

---

[19] Jesse Granspan. History.com. May 28, 2019. "7 Things You Should Know about Mount Everest."
https://www.history.com/news/7-things-you-should-know-about-mount-everest

is not for the faint of heart. It takes most climbers years of training, devotion, and preparation to reach the summit successfully.[20]

What if I told you *climbing* Mount Everest was not the most dangerous part of an expedition? In fact, the *descent* is far deadlier.

According to research published in Scientific American, 192 climbers died on Mount Everest between 1921 and 2006 after beginning the ascent from base camp (another twenty died before even getting started). Of those who made it into the "death zone," 56 percent died on their descent from the summit. Another 17 percent turn back before reaching the mountaintop, but still die on their way down. Only 15 percent actually died on their way up the mountain.

Are you surprised? Many researchers involved in the study were, too. But experts on the dynamics of mountain climbing responded differently. R. Douglas Fields, chief of nervous system development and plasticity at the National Institute of Health (NIH) is acquainted with the difficulties of mountaineering. To him, the results made perfect sense. It's "a common rule in climbing that more people die coming down than going up," Fields said. Why? Overconfidence and failure to plan. "You're spent getting to the top. You get tired, you're exhausted," Fields continued. Some climbers are under the mistaken impression that reaching the top is the hardest part of their trip. Sometimes it costs them their lives on the way down.[21]

---

[20] John Branch. *The New York Times*. December 18, 2017. "You Want to Climb Mount Everest? Here's What It Takes."
https://www.nytimes.com/2017/12/18/sports/climb-mount-everest.html

[21] Jordan Lite. *Scientific American*. December 10, 2008. "Death on Mount Everest: The Perils of the Descent."
https://blogs.scientificamerican.com/news-blog/death-on-mount-everest-the-perils-o-2008-12-10/?redirect=1

Plan for the *Entire* Journey

While people may plan for years to reach the top of Mount Everest, they often lack the forethought to prepare for the descent. The same is too often true of investors. Overconfidence and failure to plan are two of the most dangerous things I see in soon-to-be retirees when they come into my office. Planning the wrong way is another big problem, but we'll get to that later.

As I'm writing this book, the economic disaster of 2008 has just about faded from the collective memory. Some younger investors have never even heard of the economic crash of 2000. For people who lost nearly half their life's savings in one or both of those events, it's a different story. The pain is still fresh in their minds. Some have only recently recovered what they lost in the Great Recession. Some have still not recovered. And yet others may never recover entirely.

It's not because the economy never recovered. On the contrary, we've seen record highs for the stock market in recent years. The Dow Jones Industrial Average exceeded 25,000 points on January 4, 2018, for the first time ever. The Standard and Poor's 500 Index (better known as the S&P 500) and the Nasdaq Composite also reached all-time highs that year. Despite some serious wobbles, Wall Street guys are riding high.[22]

So why do I say that some may never recover their lost assets from an economic dip that's nearly ten years behind us?

Timing.

Bad timing, to be more specific. It's one of the aging investor's worst nemeses.

The 2008 market crash came as a shock. Very few people, if anyone, saw it coming. Some investors may tell you they timed its

---

[22] *Bloomberg. Fortune.* January 4, 2018. "Dow Jones Surpasses 25,000 for the First Time as Stocks Rally Despite Winter Storm."
http://fortune.com/2018/01/04/dow-jones-record-high-25000/

arrival. But if the financial community had been so savvy, more investors would have protected their assets before the crash. Perhaps it should have been obvious; the stock market trend was unsustainable. Banks haphazardly dished out mortgage loans. They were "too big to fail," so what could go wrong? Then Lehman Brothers shut down and reality set in. Another twelve major banks came within inches of filing for bankruptcy. What later became known as the housing bubble had finally popped. The stock market crashed shortly thereafter.

You've probably noticed the similarity between the 2008 market crisis and the dangers of Mount Everest. Before the recession started, everyone was concerned with making it to the proverbial mountaintop, capitalizing on an investor's paradise and making as much money as possible. Many failed to plan for when it was time to come back down. The market will always eventually go up—but not without dips along the way.

Overconfidence blinded many a smart investor. Greedy investing giants like Lehman Brothers inspired an overconfidence that permeated the financial marketplace. Sadly, when things went south, it was the unknowing individual investors who suffered the most. They were misled by supposed experts who oversold their ability to read the signs and pull out before stock prices dropped. Those experts were like Everest guides who plan only to lead their dependents to the top.

The stock market is unpredictable, especially over short periods of time (within about ten years), and that fact will remain, regardless of what any financial fortune teller claims.

Remember the couple I mentioned in the preface? They came into my father-in-law's office in 2009, shortly after things had turned for the worse. The Dow had dropped 777 points in a single day, more than ever before. Real estate prices were dismal. There were no signs of improvement soon. That couple lost much of their retirement nest egg and it took them years of extra work to recover. Bad timing caught them off guard. They were not prepared, and they didn't know it.

Some investors today are similarly ill-prepared. I have found over the years that many new clients don't understand their own risk tolerance. Some advisers have their clients fill out canned "risk tolerance questionnaires" to estimate risk tolerance. In my experience, these self-evaluative surveys just don't work. Many behavioral finance studies show investors are poor judges of their own risk tolerance.[23] In 2007, some people argued they were fine with high risk-exposure because their money was performing so well in the stock market. You can imagine how differently they felt at the end of 2008 when half their portfolio was gone. Whether they know it or not, most investors subject more of their assets to market risk than they would knowingly allow if they *truly* understood the risk involved. The stock market is a powerful and important investment vehicle, but market exposure must harmonize with investor risk tolerance.

A couple recently came to my office. Let's call them Mark and Elizabeth Schuler. They came in for a consultation at Elizabeth's request. Mark's best friend was a stockbroker who had handled the couple's investment portfolio for decades. All they wanted from me was a second opinion. If all went well, they planned to stop working within five years.

After a quick chat about their goals, I organized the mess of financial paperwork they'd brought and set about assessing their situation. As my team and I prepared their "Retirement Map

---

[23] Michael Kitces. Nerd's Eye View. September 14, 2016. "The Sorry State of Risk Tolerance Questionnaires for Financial Advisors." https://www.kitces.com/blog/risk-tolerance-questionnaire-and-risk-profiling-problems-for-financial-advisors-planplus-study/

Review," it was immediately apparent the Schulers were carrying significant market risk.

We scheduled a follow-up appointment for two weeks later. When they returned, I asked them to estimate their comfortable risk tolerance. In other words, how much of their savings could they comfortably afford to have exposed to stock market losses?

Elizabeth laughed at the question. "We're not comfortable losing *any* of it," she said.

I had to laugh too. Of course, no one *wants* to lose any of their money. But with assets housed in mutual funds, 401(k)s, and stocks, there's always going to be some measure of risk, not to mention fees to maintain such accounts. We always stand to lose something. So how much could they tolerate losing and still be okay to retire?

The Schulers had to think about that for a while. After some quick calculations and hurried deliberation, they finally came up with a number.

"I guess if we're just roughly estimating," Mark said, "I could see us subjecting about 10 percent of our retirement savings to the market's ups and downs and still being all right."

Can you guess what percentage of their assets were at risk? After a careful examination of the Schulers' portfolio, my team and I discovered *100 percent* of their portfolio was actually invested in individual stocks—an investment option with very high risk!

In fact, a large chunk of the Schulers' money was invested in Pacific Gas & Electric Company (PG&E), a utility company that has been around for over one hundred years. Does that name sound familiar? When I met with the Schulers, PG&E stock was soaring. But you may remember the company name from several 2019 news headlines in which the electric and natural gas giant was accused of negligence that contributed to 30 billion dollars' worth of damage caused by California wild fires. In the wake of that disaster, the company's stock dropped by more than 60 percent in a matter of months. That's how volatile individual stocks can be.

I believe that no one should invest this way, and it's especially dangerous for soon-to-be retirees. Mark and Elizabeth were in their sixties and looking to retire pretty quickly. With just a few more working years ahead of them, they were positioned to lose more than half of everything they had if the market tanked like it did in 2008. As you can imagine, that revelation shocked them.

Three Phases of Financial Life

The Schulers may have planned better if they understood the phases of financial life. When investors are severely caught off guard by economic downturns, it normally means they are investing according to the wrong phase of their financial lives. The three phases in chronological order are as follows:

- The Accumulation Phase
- The Preservation Phase
- The Distribution Phase

Each phase equates to a span of time and may have some degree of overlap. Let's examine each one.

When you first start working, you enter the **accumulation phase**. As the name suggests, your primary objective in the accumulation phase is to accumulate money. Complicated stuff, right? As far as investing goes, your goal is to save, save, and save some more. What's nice about the accumulation phase is your tolerance for risk. Endeavoring to make as much money as possible, people in the accumulation phase typically employ aggressive investment strategies. That means most of your money will be invested in the stock market. It can be volatile, but who cares when you're young? The return on investment is worth the risk when you're young enough to wait out stock market slumps.

In the accumulation phase, time is your friend. It's not the end of the world when stock prices fall and you lose a bit of money. You're still working. Your income sustains you, not the returns on your investments. There's plenty of time to wait for the market to recover, to regain your assets, and acquire more. If you're in the accumulation phase, you also benefit from something called "dollar-cost averaging," a process that mitigates the impact of market volatility. When the market drops, you—a young investor who makes regular contributions to your accounts—benefit from the extra buying capacity of your money. Shares are "cheap" in those years, and your portfolio can thus expand sizably. When the market comes back up, which it always has, your enlarged portfolio will earn more money in returns than before the market downturn. Over time, your portfolio's growth averages out to essentially negate market instability.

There is, however, one downside to having so much time on our side. It's easy for young investors to develop a false sense of security. With thirty working years ahead of you, it can be easy to think, "I can afford to spend some of this money now, there will be plenty of time to save later."

Not smart.

You're looking to accumulate enough money to serve as a thirty-year retirement income. It's never too early to start saving with retirement in mind. Yes, there may be several working decades ahead of you. But it takes all that time to develop a sufficient retirement nest egg. Start saving young, invest, watch it grow, and no matter what, don't touch that money!

Eventually, the aggressive investment strategies of the accumulation phase pose too much of a risk to older investors. It's only wise to keep an accumulation-first mindset until you're fifty to sixty years old. Then it's time for the preservation phase.

The **preservation phase** kicks in when you're about ten years from retirement, or, more specifically, when you're ten years from relying on your portfolio as primary income. Can you guess the primary objective of the preservation phase? Yep, to preserve the money you worked so hard to accumulate in the accumulation phase. Again, it's not complicated, but a simple theory can be hard to implement.

A big problem that I see in middle-aged investors is missing the cue to transition from an accumulation-only phase to one with preservation as its focus. It's an easy mistake to make, and the transition can be difficult to implement. It takes a well-thought-out distribution strategy plan, tax plan, and an understanding of finance that eludes some investors.

Some investors feel they'd do well to extend the accumulation phase for any number of reasons. Maybe they didn't start saving for retirement as early as they would have liked. Or maybe they're just good accumulators and don't see any reason to stop. Just to be clear, the preservation phase doesn't behoove you to start earning less money. It doesn't mean you all of a sudden neglect to achieve investment growth. It means you adjust your style of investing with the goal of reducing risk. Often, it's possible to do that without significantly decreasing investment returns, but that's a topic for a later chapter.

To illustrate the importance of transitioning between phases at the right time, consider these examples. For simplicity, let's assume each of the following people has 100 percent of his or her assets subject to market volatility—not an uncommon scenario. Now, imagine the stock market plummets and suddenly they've all lost half of their assets. What would happen to each of them?

• **John** is seventy. He's been retired for five years, but he still makes more on his investments than a normal person. During his working years, John was a billionaire mogul. Before the market turns, his net worth is $5 billion.

- **Margaret** is a fifty-year-old widow. She has four kids. Most of her children are approaching adulthood and they will be able to support themselves within a couple years. Margaret is self-employed, and she's done well for herself. Her net worth pre-stock market crash is $2 million.
- **Angie** is only thirty. She has barely gotten started in her career, let alone invested anything. Her net worth is $30,000.
- **Anthony** is sixty-three and works as a manager at a Fortune 500 company. He makes decent money, but he hasn't had a mind for investment until recently. He has about $1 million before the stock market crashes and most of that is stored in his 401(k).

Which one of the above examples is in a lot of trouble because he or she didn't transition through the phases of financial life at the right time? I'll give you a hint: It's only one of them.

John may not have transitioned through the phases of financial life, but he's certainly not in any trouble. With several billion dollars to his name, John is going to be just fine. He can afford to bend the rules a bit. If you're in a position like John's, you can probably put this book down now. If you're a billionaire, I take it you know a thing or two about investing.

Margaret will feel the sting of losing half her money, but she's not financially crippled. At fifty years old, she should only just be starting the transition to the preservation phase of her life. She still has plenty of working years ahead of her in which to recover her assets and store them in low-risk investment vehicles. And remember the principle of dollar-cost averaging. This is an opportunity for Margaret to buy assets while they're inexpensive. She's not happy to have lost some money, but it affords her a welcome opportunity to grow her portfolio as she continues to save toward retirement.

Angie will also be fine. She fares better than any of the other examples. She stands to lose little because she has little in the first place. She's young. Angie is still near the beginning of the accumulation phase. She has decades ahead of her to recover her losses and save much more.

That just leaves Anthony. Poor Anthony. At sixty-three he would like to retire in a couple of years but it's not going to happen after the stock market plunges. With all of his retirement savings allocated to stocks in a 401(k), his money is subject to extreme risk. He should never have been in that position at his age. Anthony neglected to transition to the preservation phase of his financial life. A 100 percent growth-oriented stock market strategy is an absurd percentage of risk for a sixty-three-year-old if he plans to retire anytime soon. But Anthony probably reasoned he needed to keep an accumulation-centered investment strategy because he was late to the investment game in the first place. His reasoning is understandable, but dicey. If Anthony were to retire and start drawing from his 401(k) while the market is down, the capacity of his portfolio to make more money over time will suffer. He would be required to sell twice as many shares to generate the same amount of income. This is called "cannibalizing your portfolio." Even when the market recovers, you have sold too many shares to enjoy long-term benefits. That leaves Anthony with two options: work longer than he planned, or risk depleting his retirement funds too early.

Anthony's example is not uncommon. He represents a common profile I see as a financial adviser: people who miss the transition from accumulation to preservation. When the market inevitably goes south, they're caught with their backs against the wall. The accumulation phase is dangerous. But it's okay when you're young; it represents a fantastic opportunity while retirement is still in the distant future. In your later working years, you *must* adjust your strategy to land safely at retirement.

The third and final phase of your financial life is the **distribution phase**. It's simple. It starts after you've retired, when you're living on the money you've earned and saved over the course of your working life. It's your time to rest, relax, and recreate. Some investment in growth-oriented positions is often still necessary—remember earlier when we discussed how long baby boomers are living? However, a strict view to safety is vital. Assets you've acquired over your working years are now needed for income sooner rather than later. There can be no room for serious risk. Without full-time wages, your investment protocols need to be conservative. You can't afford to lose your finite resources. Still, your distribution phase can be low-stress if you've invested smartly through the first, and more critical, two phases of your financial life.

The Rule of 100

Many financial advisers promote "The Rule of 100." You may have heard of it. Subtract your age from one hundred and that's the percentage of your money you can afford to invest in the stock market. Or you can think of it this way: turn your age into a percentage of your total assets and keep that money safe from stock market volatility. For example, if you are sixty years old, the Rule of 100 recommends that 60 percent of your wealth be housed in non-stock market investment vehicles. This "rule of thumb" is designed to estimate your risk tolerance and protect you from reckless investing. The guiding principle is sound, but the rule is a relic of outdated investment theory.

Today's economic landscape does not support yesterday's favorite investment strategies, including the Rule of 100. It just doesn't make sense anymore. When the Rule of 100 was conceived, Americans followed a more traditional journey to retirement. But, ultimately, investing should be predicated on an investor's goals and time horizons, not his or her age. If you're self-employed and expect to retire at seventy with residual income from your business, you will invest differently than the corporate businesswoman who wants to start drawing from her retirement accounts on the day of her sixty-fifth birthday. The point is, financial planning is too individual for blanket rules to accurately forecast your investment needs.

The 4 Percent Rule

Another famous (or maybe I should say infamous) investment guideline is the 4 percent rule. Retirement planning shouldn't be complicated, but there is such a thing as *too simple*, and the 4 percent rule illustrates that fact.

A more complete name for the 4 percent rule is "the 4 percent *withdrawal* rule." A guy named William P. Bengen came up with the idea about forty years ago. His objective was admirable. Bengen wanted to simplify the retirement process. He figured there must exist an ideal percentage of a brokerage account that one could annually withdraw without running out for thirty years. The retirement sweet spot, you might say.

After a respectable research effort, Bengen published his "4 percent rule" findings. Other experts would later inspect his study and identify 4.5 percent as a more accurate figure. Either way, withdrawing a fixed percentage every year only works in theory. When Bengen conducted his study, the stock market was soaring, and the economy looked like it'd never go down. Also, interest rates were much higher than in recent years. "Safe money" investments like bonds made better returns than today's retiree can expect. Under those circumstances, the 4 percent rule worked beautifully. But *only* under those circumstances.

When the United States stock market crashed in 2000, it took ten years for it to see any appreciable gains for large U.S. stocks. Finance experts call the years 2000 to 2010 the "lost decade" because economic conditions were stagnant. In a piece for *Kiplinger,* Sean McDonnel explains why the 4 percent rule falls short. He notes "Why the 4% Withdrawal Rule is Wrong," if retirees had withdrawn 4 percent a year from their retirement funds starting in 2000, their accounts, if they were invested mostly in United States stocks, would have "fallen by a third through 2010." That makes for a 29 percent chance of surviving a projected thirty years of retirement. Those are bleak odds. Of course, a properly diversified retirement portfolio that didn't depend on the United States stock market would have survived this decade without a hitch.[24]

One major shortcoming of Bengen's rule is failure to account for inflation, which we'll examine in a later chapter. But again, as with the Rule of 100, the biggest problem is assuming that concrete figures can apply to every investor. Withdrawal percentage is not nearly as relevant to an investor's success as the broader investment plan. With a poorly constructed or under-diversified investment strategy, some might expend their portfolios if they withdraw even 3 percent annually. On the other hand, a more robust plan might support 5 percent withdrawals, or more. Investor goals are important here, as well. Do investors want to leave a handsome inheritance to family and friends? Or maybe they'd rather their check to the morgue bounces? Perhaps they are somewhere in between. A sound retirement strategy won't rely on inflexible rules. It will account for a variety of individual circumstances.

---

[24] Sean McDonnell. *Kiplinger.* January 25, 2018. "Why the 4% Withdrawal Rule is Wrong." https://www.kiplinger.com/article/retirement/T037-C032-S014-why-the-4-withdrawal-rule-is-wrong.html

Modern Day Investing

Overconfidence and failure to plan are major retirement *faux pas*. But, planning the wrong way—incorrectly applying principles like the Rule of 100 or abiding by outdated standards like the 4 percent rule—will just as quickly get you in trouble.

Retirement planners have been around for a long time. But it's a mistake to think that effective retirement strategies from 1985 still apply to the twenty-first century. Interest rates are lower than ever before, and the average retiree will live longer than retirees in any of the generations past. Investment strategies, too, cannot be constant throughout your life. I wish they came with expiration dates stamped on them. But what worked for you in your thirties will likely not work as you approach retirement. Even with strategies rooted in Nobel Prize-winning economics, their application is ever evolving, and styles of implementation are improving. New strategies are invented, and old ones refined. The financial world is not static. It's a dynamic discipline. With that in mind, it's unwise to keep the same investment routine throughout your life. As you transition between phases of your financial life, you must adjust your strategies to reach your goals.

As you approach the time to crack open your retirement nest egg, your focus shifts to preservation and more stability. That's the destination. The 4 percent rule dropped the ball, but its mission was on point. You need dependable, sustainable income for decades of non-working life. That's a tall task. The 4 percent rule would have worked if the stock market climbed linearly and inflation was constant. The Rule of 100 would work if everyone needed to draw the same amount from his or her portfolio, and at the same age. Since things don't work that way, you need more sophisticated investment stratagems, ones curated toward your individual needs.

In later chapters, we'll investigate the latest retirement planning tools and techniques. But first, it's important that investors learn to avoid classic investment mistakes—especially emotional investing.

CHAPTER THREE

Use Your Gauges, Not Your Gut

Whether we like it or not, life is full of rules. We adhere to many rules without thinking about them. Some are strictly enforced; we call those rules "laws." We know not to exceed the speed limit (by too much), not to hurt people when we're upset, and not to take things from stores without paying. Those are the rules.

Other rules aren't so explicit, but we follow them, nonetheless. When we get our morning coffee, we stand at the end of the line. When shuffling through a crowd we say, "excuse me," sometimes even when we don't make physical contact. If you live in a big city, it might be rude to make eye contact or initiate conversation with strangers. If you live in the country, it might be rude *not* to make eye contact and to exchange a few words with passersby. No matter where we live or what we do, we're all governed by rules.

But then, there are some rules that seem easy to follow but prove more challenging in practice. For example, consider the rules that govern weight loss. On paper, it's simple: eat less, exercise more. We all know the rule, but it doesn't seem that easy to follow.

In the United States, in fact, we're having more difficulty than ever following weight loss rules. The obesity rate in America was on the rise for decades until it briefly plateaued a few years ago. Unfortunately, 2018 showed obesity is again on the rise. More adults are overweight or obese than ever before. The statistics for teenagers are especially alarming. If the obesity rate continues to climb, it's estimated that up to half of American teenagers will be obese by 2030.[25]

What makes it so hard to follow the simple rules of weight loss? Emotion.

According to the American Psychological Association (APA), emotion is the biggest weight loss hurdle. Unless one acts to address the emotions behind overeating, his or her efforts to lose weight could be in vain. It doesn't matter that in principle, weight loss is "simple." On the contrary, psychologists Sarah Weiss, PhD, and Nancy Molitor, PhD, said that "the causes of obesity are rarely limited to genetic factors, prolonged overeating or a sedentary lifestyle. What we do and don't do often results from how we think and feel."[26]

How we think and feel affects nearly every decision we make in life. Often, it can be to our detriment. Here's another scenario where emotion can get us into trouble. See if you can identify the "simple" rule that's hard to follow in practice.

Imagine a typical investor. Let's call him Joe. Joe is an average guy in every respect. He works a nine-to-five office job making decent money. He knows he ought to invest some of his income to build a retirement nest egg. Joe's office buddy Bill gives Joe a "tip." Or maybe a finance article pops up on his news feed. Or he hears

[25] Amy Norton. WebMD. June 12, 2018. "U.S. Obesity Rates Rising Again." https://www.webmd.com/diet/obesity/news/20180612/us-obesity-rates-rising-again#1
[26] *American Psychological Association.* 2019. "Mind/Body Health: Obesity." https://www.apa.org/helpcenter/obesity

a financial analyst make exciting claims on the radio. Regardless of the source, Joe sets his sights on a stock.

Now, Joe is a frugal man. He likes what he hears about this stock, but he's hesitant to throw his money at an unsure thing. He waits a while to verify this stock will really make him money. The share price continues to rise and build momentum, so Joe finally decides he better get in on the action.

With fingers crossed and bated breath, Joe makes his move and buys into the stock. He's optimistic. Oh, what the future might bring! Wealth and glory await him. Joe's morning routine has changed. He doesn't read the news or check social media upon waking up. No, now Joe can't do anything before checking the stock market on his phone. Every day his excitement increases as his stock climbs in value. After a week he's positively thrilled. His stock has already gone up by two dollars a share. Joe is a genius! Maybe he should quit his job to become a full-time investor!

But as we all know, the market moves in cycles, and Joe knows that, too. But he can't help feeling anxious when the market opens lower on the following Monday. His euphoria quickly fades. His stock has given back some of its gains. Tuesday is even worse. Joe's investment has nearly depreciated to its starting value. What's going on? This wasn't the plan. If the market continues to drop, Joe might even start to lose money! Now he's in denial. That simply can't happen.

It happens. His stock's value has dropped below the price at which he bought it. Denial gives way to fear, and, in turn, depression. What a disaster this has become. Every day Joe loses even more money. Should he get out now? Some retirement nest egg this is amounting to be! Joe is worse off than he was before deciding to play the investment game. He decides to give it one more day. If the market has dropped again the following morning, he'll pull the plug.

Sure enough, Joe has lost more money by the next day. In fact, his stock has tanked. Joe panics. Why did he give it another day? He knew it was only going to get worse. What a fool he was. He must get out now before he loses even more money. Joe pulls up his online trading account and drops his stock like a hot potato. Good thing too, he reasons, because the stock price has fallen even further by end of day.

After a few days, Joe's curiosity gets the better of him. He checks to see how the stock is fairing. Alas, the market is recovering! The stock he dropped is on the rise. It's gained back its losses and the radio analyst is singing its praises again. What should Joe do now? He clearly got out too early. Should he buy back in and hope to time the market more accurately this time?

And the cycle repeats.

Can you identify the simple rule Joe neglected to follow? "Buy low, sell high." It doesn't get much simpler than that, at least in writing. In practice, however . . . well, the story's point is clear. Joe may be a fictional character, but his story is far from made up. Joe's example is typical of a well-researched phenomenon. It's called the cycle of investor emotions, and it plagues the average investor.

This cycle begins with inexperienced investors' overconfidence in their stock market prowess. As *U.S. News* explains, there are many biases and misunderstandings that can financially harm even the most confident investor.[27] When such an investor takes too many risks because they believe too strongly in their personal investment decisions, this normally leads to panic over short-term losses, when investors ought to approach the stock market—and investment in general—with a view to long-term growth. "Instead of staying the course," the site continues, "emotional biases drive

[27] Rebecca Lake. *U.S. News & World Report*: Money. June 13, 2017. "The Dangers of Being an Overconfident Investor."
https://money.usnews.com/investing/articles/2017-06-13/the-dangers-of-being-an-overconfident-investor

investors to respond to the market's ups and downs in a way that harms their financial well-being."

Emotional investing was demonstrated by a study conducted by the investor research firm, Dalbar. For decades, they have compared the twenty-year average returns of the market with the twenty-year returns of the average equity fund investor. Their analysis reveals the way investors fare over the long term, something Dalbar credits in part to emotional investing.[28]

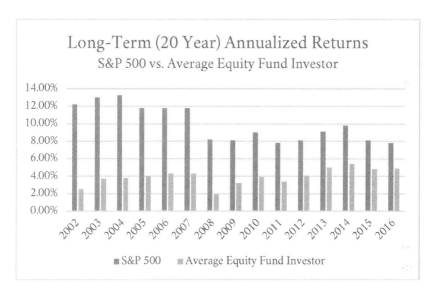

An article in Investopedia reported on the study, saying an "unmanaged S&P 500 Index earned an average of 7.81 percent annually. Over that same period, the average equity investor earned a paltry 3.49 percent annually."[29] This tells me the stock market itself performed much better than an individual, someone

---

[28] 2018. Dalbar. "2018 Quantitative Analysis of Investor Behavior."
https://svwealth.com/wp-content/uploads/2018/04/dalbar_study.pdf
[29] Thomas Smith. Investopedia. April 26, 2019. "Manage My Own Investments? Are You Kidding?"
https://www.investopedia.com/articles/stocks/08/invest-on-your-own.asp

who handles their portfolio based on their emotions. If investors had let their money accrue returns over the long run, they may have seen almost double returns. What does that mean in dollars and cents?

Let's assume our investor, Joe, puts $1,000 in the stock market. He continues to add $6,000 annually over the next twenty years. That's $121,000 invested out of pocket. Because of emotional investing and trying to time the market, Joe averages a 1.9 percent annual return, which earns him a measly $22,968 after twenty years. That's less than 20 percent of what he invested. But what if Joe had let his money sit for the same twenty years? The S&P 500 averaged an 8.4 percent gain annually over that period (we're assuming it's 1988 to 2008). Now, the $121,000 Joe invested yields $150,572 in returns, almost 125 percent total return. What a difference! And that's without any fancy investment portfolio.[30]

The moral of the story: stick to long-term investment strategies and keep emotion out of the picture. Still, that's easier said than done. Emotional investing ensnares many an individual investor, but it's powerful enough even to mislead entire economies.

Emotion Versus the World

Whenever economies crash, emotion is involved, and I don't just mean after things turn for the worse. Often, it is emotion that sinks an economy in the first place.

Over the centuries, all sorts of things have been used as currency. If you think it's crazy that the stock market operates on the idea of investors dividing ownership of companies into "shares," then you'll get a kick out of the Dutch "tulip bubble" of

---

[30] Mandi Woodruff. *Business Insider*. March 30, 2012. "We Let Emotions Wreck Our Investment Portfolio All Too Easily."
https://www.businessinsider.com/infographic-see-how-easily-we-let-emotions-wreck-our-investment-portfolio-2012-3

1637. That's right—tulip bulbs were at one point an economy's primary currency.

It all started in 1593. Tulips, native to Turkey, were introduced to the Dutch, and import to Holland began. It was a beautiful novelty and tulips quickly became a rare commodity. The Dutch elite sought after the stunning flower as a symbol of wealth and status. Soon the flower was selling for a hefty price. The tulip fervor was just getting started.

Then, something extraordinary happened. The tulips, probably due to Holland's foreign conditions, contracted a virus. It was called mosaic, and it wasn't like any other virus that you've probably heard of. Mosaic didn't kill the tulips. On the contrary, it warped their genes to produce magnificent "flames" of brilliant color. The diversity of colors seemed limitless, and the rarity of certain strains skyrocketed the flower's value. The already expensive tulip increased in value twentyfold in just a month's time. Eventually, the entire country was dealing in tulip bulbs. It had become the nation's primary currency. At the height of its value, a single tulip could be exchanged for entire estates, hereditary land, life savings—just about anything that wasn't another tulip.

It's probably not hard to see where this story is headed. The idea of staking so much on something as fragile and fleeting as a flower sounds laughable. But that's the problem with emotional investing: in the moment, it blinds investors to their follies.

The economy in Holland became a speculative bubble. In other words, its currency maintained its value based on the price people assigned to it, not on any intrinsic worth. Bubbles always pop. Eventually, some got the idea to sell their tulips for things of genuine value. A domino effect ensued. Soon, everyone was trying to sell his or her tulips and no one was interested in buying them. In turn, the price took a steep dive. The flower that could once buy houses was then worth the same as a common onion. A severe economic depression set in, and it would be a long time before the Dutch allowed speculative investment back into their country.[31]

The tulip bubble was the first of many economic bubbles that would develop and subsequently wreck world economies. Holland was a major economic hub in the seventeenth century. The decimation of its economy permeated all of Europe and the civilized world. It all started with emotional investing. What started as a pretty flower developed into a "get rich quick" scheme for opportunistic investors. Like our buddy Joe, many bought into the craze when prices had already risen, expecting prices to increase interminably. Some used borrowed money to buy up tulip bulbs, expecting their investment to yield handsome returns. Greed took over, and the price of tulips inflated beyond reason. Before long, insightful traders started to unload their tulips. Others followed and soon the market was all supply and no demand. Prices plummeted, and investors panicked.

Does that sound familiar? It's the cycle of investor emotions again. In the case of the tulip bubble of 1637, it devastated the entire world economy. If emotional investing can do that, it can more easily prevent us from reaching our financial goals and investment potential.

Learn to Trust Your Gauges

When John F. Kennedy Jr. crashed his plane off the coast of Martha's Vineyard, flight conditions were hazy but navigable. A pilot never *wants* to fly with limited visibility, but summer humidity in New England yields an almost constant foggy gauze at flight altitude. In fact, at about the same time that JFK Jr. was preparing for his flight, Flight Services told a pilot flying from

---

[31] Andrew Beattie. Investopedia. "Market Crashes: The Tulip and Bulb Craze (1630s)." https://www.investopedia.com/features/crashes/crashes2.asp

Teterboro, New Jersey, to Nantucket, Massachusetts, that conditions were not adverse. That pilot was much more experienced than John-John, though.

Spatial disorientation is the official term for the phenomenon that beset JFK Jr., and it's the pilot's greatest enemy. It can affect any pilot without warning, but it will only kill the inexperienced. More capable pilots know to use their gauges, not their guts. As it turns out, Kennedy may not have known how to use his gauges when it really counted.

Pilots undergo a rigorous instrument training course. I spent a year as a flight instructor in Alexandria, Minnesota, teaching this course to private pilots and let me tell you, it's tough. At one point, we put students "under the hood." The hood is a helmet that restricts visibility to the horizon so they can fly only with the assistance of their gauges (as the instructor, I have a yoke on the right side if they lose control—don't worry). At the time of his crash, JFK Jr. had not completed all of this training. The instruction is usually broken into three sections. First, up-and-coming pilots learn to fly based on their instruments. Second, they learn to navigate with their instruments. Third, and most importantly, when flying in instrument conditions, pilots are taught to trust their instruments *no matter what*. Even when instinct says otherwise, a pilot must be confident that the gauges are always right. John F. Kennedy Jr. had missed that critical final third of his training.[32]

Instinct is just another word for making decisions based on emotion. It's as dangerous for the investor as it is for the pilot. Well ... almost. It's not *typically* a matter of life and death, and yet some studies have shown that when it comes down to it, people will

---

[32] Phaedra Hise. *Salon.* July 15, 2000. "JFK Jr.'s Fatal Mistakes."
https://www.salon.com/2000/07/15/ntsb_3/

often choose to save their money rather than get the medical care they need. [33]

Few things impact our bodies like the stress and despair of financial hardship. Emotional investing can make the difference between the retirement of your dreams and falling short. In later chapters, we'll examine some of the "gauges" that can protect investors in more detail. For now, here are three fundamental investment rules. They're simple on paper, but many investors neglect to follow them.

1. Own Equities

According to its most basic definition, an equity is a stock. Owning equity means you share partial ownership of a company. But let me be clear, I am not advocating for an individual stock purchase, nor investment in traditional mutual funds. I encourage you to invest in index funds and asset class funds: funds where there is no forecasting component involved.

A huge advantage of these funds is lower-than-average internal expenses. In a later chapter, I'll elaborate on the importance of investing in funds with low fees. For now, suffice it to say that lower fees mean higher returns. It's not rocket science.

Index and asset class funds carry several other benefits. They have low turnover ratios, they're inexpensive and diversified, and they almost always outperform old-fashioned retail mutual funds.

2. Diversify

"Diversify!" How many times have you heard it from finance clerics yelling at you through a TV screen? I'm almost embarrassed to use the word. Its definition has been abused and obscured in the investing world. But true diversification is an essential component of investment success.

---

[33] Bruce Japsen. *Forbes.* March 26, 2018. "Poll: 44% of Americans Skip Doctor Visits Because of Cost."
https://www.forbes.com/sites/brucejapsen/2018/03/26/poll-44-of-americans-skip-doctor-visits-due-to-cost/#4be8424f6f57

Diversification is *not* owning several different investments within a portfolio. It's not simply owning "a bunch of different things." Surprised? The Wall Street guys have done a good job of spreading that definition, but it's mistaken. In 1990, Dr. Harry Markowitz published "Modern Portfolio Theory" wherein he introduced the scientific process of diversification. He was awarded a Nobel Prize for the contribution to economics.[34]

Markowitz's definition is a bit complicated, but in layman's terms, diversification means owning the correct amount of various investments that *move dissimilarly*. In other words, when the value of one investment declines, others you own are increasing in value, or decreasing at a lower rate. The result is better returns with lower risk. At the end of the day, every investor's primary goal is to make the most efficient gains with the least risk. Correct diversification would have saved a lot of investors from heartache when the stock market crashed in 2008.

3. Rebalance

To rebalance is to buy low and sell high without the emotional impediments that often shoot us in the foot. It only works if steps one and two are strictly followed. In any portfolio, a level of asset allocation should be established. Asset allocation is a strategy to balance risk and return. It varies from investor to investor. For example, an asset allocation may call for a fifty/fifty split between stocks and bonds. That means 50 percent of a target allocation contains stocks, and the other 50 percent bonds. Let's say that after some time the portfolio's stocks have performed especially well. That in turn increases the stocks' weight in the investor's asset allocation. To achieve equilibrium, the investor ought to *rebalance* by selling some stocks and buying bonds, thereby realigning with his or her target allocation.

---

[34] James Chen. Investopedia. May 21, 2019. "Modern Portfolio Theory." https://www.investopedia.com/terms/m/modernportfoliotheory.asp

Rebalancing is crucial for long-term investing, as asset allocations adjust over time. As you age, your risk tolerance changes, and you need to rebalance your portfolio to maintain an investment strategy that aligns with your present circumstances. That said, I don't advise investors to set about an extensive rebalancing of their portfolios without help from a financial professional. As you progress through retirement, your risk tolerance continues to adjust and—to some investors' surprise— risk tolerance can at times *increase* for retirees under many circumstances. Rebalancing is not always about minimizing stock presence in one's portfolio. Rather, it is to reestablish balance according to current financial conditions and an investor's position within a larger investment plan.

CHAPTER FOUR

Don't Get in Your Own Way

The world in 1936 was racked with suspense. The major nations of Europe were trepidatious. World War I was still in recent memory. It baffled experts that such an immense conflict could erupt surreptitiously, almost without warning. The most frightening consequence of their confusion was the thought that it could happen again.

To end World War I, and to prevent a second world war, the Allied Nations convened on June 28, 1919, to negotiate what would become the Treaty of Versailles. Among other impositions, the treaty required Germany to assume exclusive responsibility for the damage and loss caused by the war and it prohibited Germany from taking any future action that would hint of militaristic intent. The Germans were not present for the conception of the Versailles treaty and, originally, the country refused to sign it. Only under the threat of invasion by the Allied forces did the German government finally acquiesce and begrudgingly agree to the terms of the Treaty of Versailles.[35]

Articles 42, 43, and 44 of the Treaty of Versailles outlined what German action would constitute a "hostile act . . . calculated to disturb the peace of the World." Article 42 explicitly forbade the

---

[35] *Peace Treaty of Versailles.* "Articles 231-247 an Annexes; Reparations." https://net.lib.byu.edu/~rdh7/wwi/versa/versa7.html

Germans "to maintain or construct any fortifications either on the left bank of the Rhine or on the right bank to the west of a line drawn 50 kilometers to the East of the Rhine." In other words, the German military was not to be found anywhere near its border with France. The Locarno Treaties of 1925 added that the Rhineland should remain permanently demilitarized. It was a positive step toward the establishment of lasting peace because Germany signed the Locarno Treaties voluntarily.[36]

All seemed well in the world until 1935. On October 3, Italy invaded Ethiopia. My wife, Brittany, and I have traveled to Ethiopia four times, and two of our sons were adopted from there. The country has a rich culture and a tumultuous history of contention with hostile invaders. Italy is among the most recent to have made claim to Ethiopia's people and resources. The League of Nations had expressly forbidden Italy's attempts at conquest, but the Mediterranean power was not fazed. The world launched into an uproar. The new German government, led by a certain Adolf Hitler, capitalized on this opportunity to make its own military moves in violation of international law. On March 7, 1936, the German army remilitarized the Rhineland.

Such flagrant disrespect for the Treaty of Versailles and the Locarno Treaties should have been met with a swift countermeasure. And yet, eight months later, on November 12, Britain and France had done nothing to squash the German threat. On that day, Winston Churchill took his place before Parliament and delivered a speech that would prove veritably prophetic.

Churchill was not Prime Minister in 1936. In fact, he was at perhaps the lowest point in his political career. He had little power and he was frustrated with those who had more. In his speech to Parliament, he accused those tasked with defending the country of

---

[36] Martin Gilbert and Richard Gott. *The Appeasers*. First Edition. London, United Kingdom. Phoenix. 1963.

"go[ing] on in strange paradox." It was a time to act. Instead, the country's leaders "decided only to be undecided, resolved to be irresolute, adamant for drift, solid for fluidity, all-powerful to be impotent." The British and their allies were allowing the German threat to go unchecked and sat idly by, negligent, while the threat of global conflict grew before their eyes. Churchill finally delivered the following scalding denunciation: "The era of *procrastination*, of half-measures, of soothing and baffling expedients, of delays, is coming to its close. In its place we are entering a period of consequences."[37]

Eventually, the consequence of procrastination rears its head. In the case of Britain's delayed response to German military action, World War II broke out. Granted, more was involved in the development of history's greatest war. Still, procrastination was an avoidable contributor.

As investors, our procrastination isn't going to set nations at war. But it can limit our retirement potential. I get it; it's easy to neglect our financial future when we're busy living life. We don't want to waste the present stressing about the future. But at some point, the period of procrastination transitions to a period of consequences and we must deal with the results of our negligence. It's much better to plan a little now and enjoy the benefits of long-term investment growth when retirement rolls around.

Procrastination Nation

If you consider yourself a procrastinator, take solace in knowing you're not alone. Not at all. It's such a big problem that psychologists have studied it for centuries. Even Sigmund Freud endeavored to isolate a root cause for procrastination. (In typical Freudian fashion, he attributed it to stunted development during

---

[37] RML. January 12, 2015. "'The Prophet Churchill': Paris 2015."
https://richardlangworth.com/paris2015

toilet training. What was up with that guy?)[38] Since then, different strains of psychology have chalked it up to a range of contributing factors. Early theories suggested neuroses and self-hatred, as if procrastinators guarantee their own failure to derive some sick mentally masochistic pleasure. Later, psychologists decided that was far-fetched, and they softened their stance. Rather than neurotic, procrastinators were just lazy and incapable of motivating themselves. Eventually, that theory went out of vogue as well. These days, psychologists can only agree that they don't really know of any fundamental source of procrastination. However, they have done a good job of outlining the typical procrastinator's dilemma.[39]

Psychologists identify procrastination as an "avoidance behavior." Why procrastinators want to avoid a task is uncertain. It may not seem important enough to warrant the procrastinator's time. Or, conversely, it may be so important that anxiety and dread set in. In the latter case, avoidance behavior becomes a detrimental coping mechanism in which people "give in to feel good," according to Timothy Pychyl, a professor who studies procrastination at Carleton University. Many rationalize they perform better under pressure, but research suggests that is almost never true.[40] Still, procrastinators often find themselves "cramming" as important deadlines approach.

Some may be capable of cramming successfully, like Tim Urban, a blogger and TED Talk speaker who didn't start his

---

[38] Susan Krauss Whitbourne, Ph.D. *Psychology Today*. January 9, 2018. "A New Way to Understand Procrastination."
https://www.psychologytoday.com/us/blog/fulfillment-any-age/201801/new-way-understand-procrastination
[39] Ibid.
[40] Timothy A Pychyl Ph.D. *Psychology Today*. April 25, 2008. "Giving in to Feel Good: Why Self-Regulation Fails."
https://www.psychologytoday.com/us/blog/dont-delay/200804/giving-in-feel-good-why-self-regulation-fails

ninety-page senior college thesis until seventy-two hours before it was due—and he finished it. The vast majority are not such capable procrastinators. With investing, however, it doesn't make a difference. There is no opportunity to "cram." It takes time to accumulate a retirement nest egg and there's no way around that.[41]

Let's examine two hypothetical investors. The first is a free spirit. For the most part, he lives life on a whim. We'll call him James. His twin sister, Amy, is the opposite. She is strait-laced and does things by the book. From childhood, Amy knew her life plan and stuck to it. How does each fare when it's time to retire?

James. After graduating from high school, James decides to forego college and gets a job with an elevator services company, installing and repairing elevator cars. He works with that company for eight years before deciding to travel the world. Each year, James had contributed $5,000 to an IRA, but then he stops. When he quits his job, James has invested $40,000 total for retirement. He fails to add anything more for the duration of his working life.

Amy. Amy always dreamed of becoming a lawyer and fighting for the little guy. After high school, she pursues her dream and attends law school. After passing the bar and getting her career off the ground, Amy starts investing at age twenty-six. She follows her brother's lead and invests $5,000 a year in an IRA. Unlike James, though, Amy continues to add $5,000 annually for the length of her career. When she decides to retire at sixty-five, Amy has invested $200,000 compared to James' $40,000.

If James and Amy earn the same rate of return, who has a bigger retirement nest egg at age sixty-five? Obviously, it's Amy, right?

Nope. And it's not even that close.

---

[41] Tim Urban. Ted. February 2016. "Inside the Mind of a Master Procrastinator." https://www.ted.com/talks/tim_urban_inside_the_mind_of_a_master_procrastinator ?language=en

How can that be? Let's assume both earn 10 percent annually on their investments. On the day of their sixty-fifth birthdays, James will have accumulated $2,587,899. Amy's portfolio totals $2,212,963. How could James have retired with nearly $400,000 more than Amy when he seemed to have invested so immaturely?

Remember, we're talking about procrastination. James left much to be desired as an investor profile goes. But he did one thing right: he started investing young.

Now, this isn't meant to be a commentary on college or career path. The point is, a few years of extra investment can make a tremendous difference by the time retirement rolls around. The time value of money cannot be underestimated. Compounding interest is the name of the game for investors. Interest needs *time* to compound. If a twenty-year-old wants to have raised $100,000 by the time he retires, he only needs to invest $1,372 today (we're keeping our assumption of 10 percent annual interest). A fifty-year-old would need to invest $24,000 to achieve the same result.

This isn't meant to sound discouraging. Some investors panic when they feel they don't have "enough time" to save enough. But whatever your current age, the best time to start investing is *now*. Get started today and you may be surprised to see how much a well-designed financial plan can do for your retirement prospects.

Overspending

Overspending is a product of procrastination. Procrastinators would rather live for the present than consider the future. Overspending derives from that attitude. That's not to say that we should deprive ourselves of a happy life now just to maximize our retirement income. My objective is to help people live richly, not die wealthy. But some would-be investors feel their incomes can't support much in the way of savings. Many of my clients used to subscribe to that erroneous notion.

One couple was especially adamant: they could not afford to save *anything*. The couple, whom we'll call Matt and Joyce, made about $60,000 in combined income, *and* they were raising two children. Their situation matches that of the average American family. During one of our first meetings together, we sat down to see where they might procure some savings.

"Honestly," the wife said, "I don't see how we can afford to save anything at all. It's not like we live extravagantly. We haven't even taken a vacation in the last five years; we just can't afford it."

I felt for her. Many find themselves in the same position. The idea of retirement savings is little more than wishful thinking. I asked the couple to describe their daily routine.

"Well our first priority is to get the kids up and ready for school," said the husband. "I normally throw breakfast together while Joyce gets the kids washed up and dressed. After they're on the bus and off, we only have a few minutes to get ourselves together and leave for work. On the way I normally grab a coffee somewhere and then I'm at work until five . . ."

I stopped him there and asked Joyce if she drank coffee, too. Sure enough, she was in the habit of stopping for coffee on her way to work as well. We pulled out the calculator and did some quick math. Matt drank his coffee black, but Joyce liked her coffee with a few more frills. Between the two of them, they spent about $10.50 on coffee *every day*.

Now, a daily coffee hardly constitutes extravagant expense. But if we assume each month has twenty-two working days, and Matt and Joyce each bought a coffee on their way to work every day of the year, they would have spent $2,772 on coffee alone. That's more than 5 percent of their total income after taxes! Just by brewing their coffee at home, Matt and Joyce could invest about 5 percent of their income each year. From that small adjustment, they could reposition themselves to retire within striking distance of a million dollars.

Overspending often conjures the idea of incorrigible shopaholics maxing out credit card limits. But it's rarely so extreme. If we carefully examine our spending habits, we'll probably find areas, however small, where we can cut back. It's easy to write off small spending as inconsequential. If we redirect those funds for investment, however, it can tremendously bolster our financial portfolio.

Wrap-Up

In this first section, we've identified the modern-day investor. We've established what investors need to accomplish for a successful retirement. We've also addressed the common *internal* obstacles investors face: emotional investing, procrastination, and overspending. It'd be nice if we only needed to adjust our personal investment creed to succeed as investors. Unfortunately, though, many *external* inhibitors exist that threaten to undermine our financial goals. The next section will address those.

Section Two:

Key Financial Principles

Reality leaves a lot to the imagination.

—JOHN LENNON

CHAPTER FIVE

Keep a Weather Eye out for Hidden Fees

S ometimes, investors do everything right. They own equities, diversify their portfolios correctly, and rebalance to capitalize on dissimilar price movement. Still, for some reason, they don't see the returns they expect. It seems like something chips away at their potential earnings.

The culprit is often hidden fees.

When I was first thinking about this chapter, I happened to be flying to one of our offices in Bismarck, North Dakota, the location my father-in-law heads up. It reminded me of a cautionary tale I'd heard early in my career as a pilot. The bizarre story illustrates how hidden fees can get you.

If you're a fan of Morrisey, The Smiths' former front man, you may be familiar with the singer's pointedly named song, "Munich Air Disaster 1958." The title is a bit on the nose, but it's a decent homage to victims of the 1958 British European Airlines (BEA) flight 609 crash.

On February 6, 1958, The BEA flight crashed right after takeoff. At least that's what one newspaper reported in the immediate wake of the disaster. It seems more likely that the plane never left the ground at all. Twice, Captain James Thain, the thirty-seven-year-old pilot, attempted to take off. Twice, he abandoned the effort, reporting engine difficulty.

"On the runway it was decided that the engines were entirely satisfactory," claimed a BEA statement issued days after the incident. "The aircraft then went out to the end of the runway again for take-off . . . It overshot the runway and hit a house 300 yards from the end of the runway with its port wing. It then veered to the right, hit a hut, and burst into flames."[42]

Twenty-one people died in the accident; another two died later from the injuries they sustained. As airplane crashes go, the casualties were minimal. The accident was an international spectacle, though, because eight among the dead were Manchester United soccer team players (this is probably an inappropriate place to add that I rather dislike "Man U" but . . . Visca el Barca!).

An investigation was launched to identify the issue. What had turned a routine flight into a fatal disaster? Had maintenance been negligent during its inspection of the engines? The captain had felt some drag. Maybe the engines were not safe for take-off after all. Nope—later inspection deemed engine failure a nonfactor.

Maybe it was a problem with the wings. Some photos taken before the crash showed icy buildup. Evidently, it was the pilot's responsibility to check for that, and so Captain Thain—who survived the incident—was charged with criminal negligence. But

---

[42] The Guardian Research Department. *The Guardian*. May 28, 2011. "7 February 1958: Seven of United's Players Killed: Matt Busby Seriously Hurt in Munich Air Crash." https://www.theguardian.com/media/from-the-archive-blog/2011/may/28/munich-manchester-united-busby-1958

ice on the wings was not the problem either, and the courts later exonerated Thain.[43]

No, the problem was nothing as major and obvious as engine problems and wing interference.

It was slush.

A bit of slush had accumulated near the end of the runway and it slowed the plane just as it was reaching rotation speed—the speed at which an aircraft lifts off the ground.

Sometimes it's the little things that crash the plane. No one thought to check the runway for slush, at least not before BEA flight 609 claimed twenty-three lives. Hidden fees are like the slush that unhinge our retirement plans, even when we've accounted for every major financial obstacle. They may seem like a pesky inconvenience, but hidden fees compounded over time can severely undercut your retirement nest egg.

Read the Fine Print

Hidden fees and undetected charges can pose a serious threat to our investments if we don't vigilantly stave them off. "Hidden" is the operative word here. They may sneak up on us, but they're not entirely undisclosed. That would be illegal, and banks, mutual funds, and the like are too smart to behave illegally. Instead, they bury extra fees in pages of fine print hoping we won't notice. Often, they're right. It's so much easier to skip through the paperwork and just pay.

When's the last time you read the terms and conditions when downloading new software or updating your phone? I normally scroll to the bottom as quickly as I can and click "I agree" without

---

[43] History.com Editors. History.com. August 21, 2018. "Man United Players among Victims of Plane Crash."
https://www.history.com/this-day-in-history/man-united-players-among-victims-of-plane-crash

a second thought. So far, it hasn't gotten me in trouble. The worst that's happened is some features on my phone change and others disappear. Where our money is concerned, we stand to lose a lot more. Big companies hope that we'll treat their fine print with the same hurried inattention to detail. Banks slip in maintenance and transaction fees. Phone companies disguise service fees and surcharges. Even grocery stores are getting in on the charade!

Have you ever looked at the food products you've bought for years and wondered if they're getting smaller? Well, you're not losing your mind. In fact, a 2008 article entitled "Hidden Price Increases at the Grocery Store" examined that very phenomenon (while it's a bit dated, tell me if you think the principle *isn't* still at play today). A yogurt container shrinks from eight ounces to six, but the price stays the same. Ah, that's the rub! Likewise, fabric softeners quietly removed 10 percent of the sheets from boxes; ice cream cartons shrunk by 12 percent; ketchup bottles by 9 percent. Who do these manufacturers think they're dealing with? Naïve shoppers who don't care enough to mind the details? Well, yeah. And their deception has all but flown under the radar.[44]

Undeclared fees are hidden everywhere in the investment world and many imprudent investors have unknowingly sacrificed their hard-earned money. A few investment options are especially guilty of including hidden fees. We'll talk about the five most common offenders:

1. Mutual funds
2. 401(k)s
3. Brokerage accounts
4. Non-traded REITs and private placement investments
5. Variable annuities

---

[44] J.D. Roth. *Get Rich Slowly.* July 29, 2008. "Hidden Price Increases at the Grocery Store." https://www.getrichslowly.org/hidden-price-increases-at-the-grocery-store/

Hidden Fees in . . . Mutual Funds

Mutual funds can be dangerous in many ways. An index or asset class fund can be a wise investment choice and yield respectable returns. Those returns can quickly disappear, however, to pay unexpected trading (or transaction) costs. According to Lorraine Ell, the CEO of Better Money Decisions, trading costs are the invisible culprit that erodes mutual fund returns.

In her article, "Beware of Hidden Costs Lurking in Your Mutual Fund Portfolio," Ell identifies the heart of the problem: "Small increases in fund expense ratios can add up to big dollar differences in your returns over time. For example, let's look at two funds: a $10,000 investment in a fund with a 2 percent expense ratio compared with the same $10,000 investment in a fund with a 0.5 percent expense ratio. If both have gains of 10 percent in a year, the fund with the higher expense would net $10,800 vs. $10,950 for the fund with lower expenses. That difference compounds over time."

To put this in plain English, Ell is saying the more it costs to operate a mutual fund, the less money goes back into an investor's pocket. Each fee is a drain on the ability of your investments to make money.

Another phenomenon of mutual funds is, when a fund buys or sells large amounts of a company's stock, it, in effect, shifts the market. In other words, the activity of a mutual fund can have such an impact on the stock market itself that share prices rise or fall accordingly. That often means a mutual fund is still buying up stock even as it forces market prices up, or conversely, it is selling stock while contributing to the fall in prices.[45]

---

[45] Lorraine Ell. *Kiplinger*. June 11, 2018. "Beware of Hidden Costs Lurking in Your Mutual Fund Portfolio!"
https://www.kiplinger.com/article/investing/T041-C032-S014-beware-of-hidden-costs-in-your-mutual-funds.html

If that's still confusing, don't worry. Here's the bottom line: the average mutual fund investor pays 1.44 percent in costs every year *whether they receive positive returns or not.* When a mutual fund is performing well, it's easy to write fees off as the "cost of doing business." But that pill gets a little harder to swallow when a mutual fund is losing money.

Now, just to be clear, mutual fund commissions are always disclosed in the prospectus. But those disclosures can be misleading—it seems as though one needs a law degree to understand a mutual fund's fine print. It's no mistake that the language is difficult to comprehend. The average investor gets lost before making it through page one, and that's the way mutual funds like it. It's in their best interest for us to remain in the dark.[46]

The investment firm Rebalance IRA conducted a survey in 2014 to gauge investor awareness. The results of its study were published in the article, "The Investment Fees You Don't Realize You're Paying," in U.S. News and World Report. According to the study's findings, most mutual fund investors don't know they're paying extra fees.[47]

The survey polled 1,165 baby boomers. They all worked full-time jobs, and they were all investing in mutual funds. When asked how much they were paying in investment fees, 46 percent said they weren't paying any fees at all. Another 19 percent knew they paid fees, but they reported the total came to less than 0.5 percent, as far as they knew. In fact, they were averaging about 1.5 percent in annual fees.

---

[46] Beverly Goodman. *Barron's.* March 2, 2013. "The Hidden Cost of Doing Business." https://www.barrons.com/articles/SB50001424052748704356104578326293404837 234

[47] Kate Stalter. *U.S. News & World Report.* December 15, 2014. "The Investment Fees You Don't Realize You're Paying." https://money.usnews.com/money/personal-finance/mutual-funds/articles/2014/12/15/the-investment-fees-you-dont-realize-youre-paying

Somewhere, there is a disconnect. It's not that investors are uneducated or flippant in their investment decisions. Rather, mutual funds are *deliberately* wily. To avoid hidden fees in mutual funds, keep these points in mind:

Make an investment strategy and *stick to it*. There are a myriad of mutual fund options, but it's unwise to move money frequently in pursuit of marginally better returns. There will always be another mutual fund performing better at a given moment. But remember, we're interested in long-term growth. Once you've identified your goals and risk tolerance and found a strategy that supports them, don't change it!

Investment type matters. There are taxable and non-taxable accounts. It's important to know the difference and evaluate which type best fits your investment goals. Each has benefits and drawbacks but, as with fees, taxable accounts with a high level of trading will cost you the most.

Understand clearly how your financial adviser gets paid. The term "financial adviser" gets thrown around and its meaning has been heavily obscured. Some "advisers" are, in fact, traditional stockbrokers. They're paid a commission every time they make a trade. Others are Registered Investment Advisers or Investment Adviser Representatives who receive either a percentage of assets or a flat fee. You should work with the latter. Registered Investment Advisers are registered with the Securities Exchange Commission (SEC). Of the 310,000 financial advisers in America, only about 30,000 are investment advisers and of them, fewer than 6,000 are not "dually registered" as a broker. If you can find one of the 6,000, you'll be starting off on the right foot.[48]

---

[48] Kelly O'Mara. RIABiz. November 11, 2015. "How Many RIAs Are There? No Seriously, How Many?"
https://riabiz.com/a/2015/11/11/how-many-rias-are-there-no-seriously-how-many

Read the fine print, and make sure you understand it. This point may seem obvious, but the *understanding* part is critical. For example, Goodman references a mutual fund statement that, at quick glance, appears to charge .375 percent in annual fees. Except, the prospectus didn't explicitly say "annual." Upon closer inspection, and further reading, it was revealed that .375 percent was *per quarter*. That amounts to a heftier 1.5 percent per year.

Do you know the differences between Class A, B, C, R and I mutual funds? If not, learn them. Watch out for 12-b1 fees. They're built into most mutual funds, but make sure you know what you're paying. Internal expense ratios are another important determinant of mutual fund value; the lower the cost, the more you get to keep.[49]

Understand whether a mutual fund is trying to "beat the market" through stock picking and forecasting or "efficiently capture the market." You will pay more in fees to a mutual fund that tries to beat the market. Data indicates that over 85 percent of the time, you pay more fees for underperforming returns. Consistently beating the market over extended periods has proven to be a tall task.

Putting Theory into Practice

Recently, I've been working with a couple who just retired. They love the outdoors and national parks. When they found out a senior pass program allows U.S. residents over sixty-two to visit more than 2,000 recreation areas in the country, they promptly retired to sunny Arizona. The husband has some health issues that are improved by Arizona's dry climate. They're loving their new retired life and living it to the fullest. They've worked hard their

---

[49] David John Marotta. *Forbes*. April 23, 2019. "Know Your Fund Expense Ratios." https://www.forbes.com/sites/davidmarotta/2019/04/23/know-your-fund-expense-ratios/#45ff4b6424ef

entire lives, and although they don't consider themselves wealthy, they built a respectable $500,000 portfolio.

Let's use this couple to illustrate how mutual funds can eat away at investor returns. Let's say their half-million-dollar portfolio is invested in expensive retail mutual funds that charge fees of 2 to 3 percent annually. That's $20,000 to $30,000 a year. Imagine if they didn't know they were paying so much in fees. If they could adjust their investment structure to cut yearly fees in half—still relatively expensive at 1 to 1.5 percent—they'd get an extra $10,000 to $15,000 every year. That is already a massive savings. Compounded over thirty years of retirement investing, they stand to gain—or lose—$450,000 or more.

Have you ever realized flight times traveling between destinations often change depending on the direction of your flight? Flying east from the United States to Europe might take six hours, but the return flight often takes seven or eight hours. What's going on? Headwinds are affecting the plane's groundspeed. The engines are putting forth the same amount of thrust in both directions, but you just can't reach your destination in the same time with pesky headwinds slowing you down. Fees and expenses are the "headwinds" of the investment world. You may do everything right, but hidden fees and costs can still prevent you from reaching your destination as quickly as you expected.

The problem is that for too long costs have become "a crucial part of the [investing] equation." So said the late John Bogle, founder of The Vanguard group, an investment management company and one of the largest providers of mutual funds in the world. Although Vanguard sells mutual funds, Bogle was quick to admit the system is designed to make the management company rich, not the individual investor. That's how any business works, "but it's not right for this business," he said in an April 2013 Frontline/PBS documentary. Bogle was an American hero for his efforts to minimize the expense of investment. His company has some pricey active mutual funds, but most of their offerings fall into the "passive" category, also known as index funds or exchange-traded funds, generally funds that capture the market with low costs by tracking an index rather than demanding high fees to try to beat the market. "What happens in the fund business is that the magic of compound returns is overwhelmed by the tyranny of compounding costs," said Bogle. In other words, if we're not careful, increasing costs can render the returns on our portfolios valueless.[50]

It's hard to isolate a complete solution to the problem of hidden fees in mutual funds. Ideally, you wouldn't have to pay fees at all, but that's unrealistic. Expelling ignorance is a good start toward maximizing your returns. With a bit of strategic planning you can minimize fees and add to the value of your retirement portfolio. A good financial planner can help you identify how to make such adjustments. "What do you do when you identified and tallied these expenses?" asks John Wasik of Forbes. ". . . ask how they can reduce the total cost to you. You can usually get a better deal, but you have to ask."[51]

Hidden Fees in . . . 401(k)s

Since July 1, 2012, 401(k) plan administrators have been legally required to provide employees with details of the fees they're paying. That's all well and good, but has the so-called 401(k) fee disclosure law increased employee cognizance?

Not really.

---

[50] Marcela Gavira and Martin Smith. Frontline/PBS. April 23, 2013. "The Retirement Gamble."
https://www.pbs.org/wgbh/frontline/film/retirement-gamble/
[51] John Wasik. *Forbes*. October 9, 2018. "Is Your 401(k) Loaded with Hidden Expenses?"
https://www.forbes.com/sites/johnwasik/2018/10/09/is-your-401k-loaded-with-hidden-expenses/#6a10a8d1757a

According to a MarketWatch article, "Everything You Need to Know About 401(k) Fees," *most* people have no idea that their retirement accounts charge fees. In fact, in a sad commentary on twenty-first century priorities, "more Americans know how much they pay for streaming services than how much they pay for their 401(k) plans." A study conducted by TD Ameritrade found a dismal 27 percent of investors knew what they were paying in 401(k) fees. By comparison, 95 percent of the same investors knew exactly what they were paying for subscriptions like Netflix and Hulu. That study was conducted in 2018; it doesn't seem like the 2012 401(k) fee disclosure law has been effective in dispelling investor ignorance.[52]

Unfortunately, 401(k)s can be much costlier than entertainment streaming services. These plans often include fees for record-keeping, administrative work, and several other charges that vary from plan to plan. Those fees, in turn, eat away at long-term investment earnings.

Typical 401(k) plans, which usually comprise mutual funds, impose fees as a percentage of the total account balance. Some can be as low as 1 percent, but an analysis by Brightscope found some plans charge an absurd 3.5 percent! The difference may not seem large at first glance, but it can amount to several hundreds of thousands of dollars over an investor's lifetime. "You should know you can pay much less [than 1 percent] because the 401(k) business has never been more competitive than in recent years," said Wasik. "Few want to get into the weeds when it comes to 401(k) expenses.

---

[52] Alessandra Malito. *MarketWatch*. April 7, 2018. "Everything You Need to Know about 401(k) Fees."
https://www.marketwatch.com/story/everything-you-need-to-know-about-401k-fees-2018-03-30

But it always make [sic] sense for you to vet your plan, since fees eat into your retirement kitty."[53]

With 401(k)s, you may wonder why it matters that anyone know the fees he or she is paying. Employers have a 401(k) plan and that's what employees get. There isn't as much room to adjust as with more general self-directed accounts. That's true, in part, but you may not be paying the same fees as your buddy a few offices down. Within the same 401(k) plan, employees can own different funds. For example, owning index funds will probably cost you less in fees than owning active funds. Ultimately, you must know what you're paying before you can weigh the value of your 401(k) and decide whether you should adjust.

Hidden Fees in . . . Brokerage Accounts

Imagine sitting down for dinner at a restaurant. You look over the menu briefly and decide that you want a burger. The menu has several options, but you're not that hungry. The most basic option will suffice. To your pleasant surprise, the burger costs just $5! The waiter takes your order and asks if the standard lettuce, tomato, and pickles are good for you. "Sounds good," you reply. The meal is good and at the end of your night you ask for the check. Wait a minute, your burger cost $25?! That can't be. You ask to see the menu again, and this time you read it more carefully. Next to the burger's price is an asterisk. At the bottom of the page, in tiny print, you read that lettuce, tomato, and pickles cost $2 extra each. Another asterisk takes you to the back of the menu where you learn your water cost you $3 and each of your two refills was $2. To have a waiter deliver your food to the table cost another $2. And finally, the restaurant automatically tacks a 25

[53] John Wasik. *Forbes*. October 9, 2018. "Is Your 401(k) Loaded with Hidden Expenses?" https://www.forbes.com/sites/johnwasik/2018/10/09/is-your-401k-loaded-with-hidden-expenses/#6a10a8d1757a

percent tip onto every order, bringing your grand total to $25, before tax.

All right, so that example got a little out of hand, but it's not far off from how stockbrokers and brokerage firms advertise their fees. You've probably seen the comparison tables that brokerage firms publish. They're supposed to inform investors and assist in finding a talented and reasonably priced stock broker. When it's all said and done, comparison tables are just another sneaky advertising strategy. The firm that publishes the table you're reading will always come out on top as the best option—at least, if you don't read the fine print and follow the asterisks. For example, Brokerage Firm A, which publishes the table, may advertise a $10 transaction fee. Its competition, Brokerage Firm B, supposedly charges $15 for the same service. Upon closer inspection, however, you find Brokerage Firm A charges extra to deal with a real person. It costs extra to have your money deposited into an account. Oh, and don't let your account sit for too long or you'll need to pay an "inactivity fee." So, is Brokerage Firm A *really* the best option? At first glance, it looks like at least the *cheapest* option. But the fine print often reveals a different story.

Hidden Fees in . . . REITs and Private Placements

Real estate investment trusts (REITs) are some of the worst offenders when it comes to hidden fees and expenses. In a later chapter, I'll discuss REITs more generally and how they are sometimes applied to diversified portfolios. Investors interested in real estate assets often like REITs for the opportunity to invest in specifically targeted passive real estate. It often yields higher returns than direct investments in real estate. The hidden fees in private non-traded REITs, however, are often downright shady. Most individual investors cannot log into their online brokerage accounts and choose to invest in this subset of REITs. More often than not, they are only accessible through a broker dealer or other licensed financial representative.

If you choose to pursue a non-traded REIT, your broker will almost definitely charge an upfront commission, which may range from 5 to 10 percent of the investment amount. However, there are additional investment fees most brokerage statements fail to mention. Say you invest $500,000 in a non-traded REIT. The statement you'll get from your broker will probably list the investment amount as $500,000. But here's the catch: They can take a chunk of that cash as payment to a salesperson (the broker) and classify it as part of the larger investment. In addition, there are loan origination fees, real estate brokerage commissions, land development costs, and broker dealer kickbacks. When all is said and done, it isn't uncommon to see just 80 to 85 percent of your total investment actually "in the ground." It may be that only $400,000 of your $500,000 is actually invested in real estate, but you're none the wiser due to devious legalese and confusing brokerage contracts.

In response to the realization that many REITs were dubiously eroding returns, disclosure laws were created to show a more transparent log of entry costs upon the purchase of a non-traded REIT. As a result, stock brokers had a more difficult time selling their junky REITs. As REITs declined in popularity, brokers turned to Private Placements (PPs) as the hot new investment.

Private placements, which are securities sold as private equity rather than as part of a public offering, are often quite similar to REITs and they can likewise be riddled with hidden fees. Many PPs are still based in real estate. They look, walk, and talk like REITs. So, what makes them different? They come with a big catch: Private placements are registered differently than REITs and they're less regulated. Important disclosures that REITs must now include are legally omitted from private placement contracts. If that sounds shady to you, you'd be right—but it is what it is.

Private placements are often advertised as cheaper alternatives to comparative public offerings, but unexpected fees can negate their apparent benefits. Hidden costs often include carried interest, monitoring costs, and portfolio company fees—none of which are reported among investment expenses. Carried interest is the terminology for a percentage of profits that get paid to the fund manager for performance. It is especially severe, and if a placement is part of a hedge fund, it can be even worse than a "standard" carried interest. Something called the "2 and 20" rule typically applies: A private placement comes with 2 percent annual fees, and 20 percent of profits are withheld as a "performance fee," or the carried interest. You might expect that, given these extreme fee structures, hedge funds would outperform less expensive strategies, right? Wrong. Hedge funds have been shown in many studies to deliver lower returns, higher fees, and less liquidity than comparable investments. To make things even worse, private equity firms sometimes classify the 20 percent performance fee such that it is not reported among investment costs. Sound criminal? It ought to be, but for now such fraudulent business practices remain legal.

Hidden Fees in . . . Variable Annuities

Variable annuities, like 401(k)s and IRAs, allow invested money to grow tax-deferred. That's about where the similarities end, however. Annuities originate in the insurance industry and come with some unique features and fees. Variable annuities' fees often range between 3.5 and 4.5 percent annually, making them one of the most expensive investment options. Of course, these fees are often hidden and line-itemed nowhere on your statement. I'll discuss the ins and outs of annuities a bit more later in this book, but for now, let me outline some of the expenses that come with variable annuities.

• **Mortality and expense fees:** Insurance companies deduct maintenance fees that may come at a flat rate or as a percentage of your annuity's total value. The maintenance fee is designed to cover record keeping and administrative expenses. Altogether, these fees will probably cost 1.5 to 2 percent of your annuity's value annually.

• **Fund fees:** These include management fees, administrative fees, and expenses incurred from sub-accounts—similar to mutual funds, but inside the annuity. The fee amount will depend entirely on your specific annuity and can range from reasonable to absurdly expensive. These typically average 1 percent per year but can go as high as 2 percent annually. You may think management fees and administrative fees sound like the same thing, but before you make that assumption, keep in mind insurance companies rarely overlook an opportunity to charge more money.

• **Additional Feature Fees, a.k.a. "Rider Charges:"** Any special feature that comes with your annuity will undoubtedly demand extra payment. Guaranteed Minimum Income Benefits (GMIB), Guaranteed Withdrawal Benefits (GWB), Enhanced Death Benefits (EDB), Long-Term Care (LTC), and a slew of others will tack on another 0.5 percent to 2.5 percent. It adds up quickly.

• **Earning Caps:** If you know anything about annuities, you're probably familiar with the concept of annuity floors, which is a provision by which your balance can never decrease in value even in years when the market dips. But did you know that some annuities can even come with a cap as well? It normally comes as a percentage, like 12 percent. An annuity with a 12 percent cap will not earn more than that even in years when the market performs well. Of course, your investment still earns more than 12 percent, but the insurance company keeps the extra.

Kill the Middleman!

There's one more hidden fee I especially resent. I harbor a personal disdain for investment firms that hire "middlemen" to do their jobs. At the start of my career in finance, I worked for a broker dealer. It didn't take long for me to realize there were profound issues with the traditional broker dealer platform, and they were all at the client's expense, literally!

Do you know what a TAMP is? It stands for "third-party asset management program." Depending on whom you ask, you may hear that it stands for "turnkey asset management program." TAMPs are to financial advisers what travel agencies have become to most travelers—they occupy a useless position between consumers and the products they want. With the advent of online travel sites like Orbitz and Travelocity, it's hard for the average person to justify the cost of a travel agent. So then why is it okay for some "financial advisers" to pawn off their responsibilities to a third-party management company that will add to clients' fees? Most TAMPs will charge clients (albeit through the financial adviser and unbeknownst to most regular investors) about 0.5 to 1 percent per year of their total returns. That's an extraordinary fee for a service that doesn't benefit clients in any way.

Advisers who use TAMPs know the idea won't sit well with their clients. To protect their firms and reputations, they sometimes hide the TAMP fees in "fund of fund" structures, burying the middleman's fee within dozens of pages of fine print.

Before committing to work with a financial adviser, ask explicitly if his or her firm uses a TAMP to handle its day-to-day account management. If the answer is "yes," you may not be getting the first-class service you expect. Many advisers do very little comprehensive financial planning. So, if they aren't doing financial and tax planning themselves, and they aren't managing your investments, what exactly *are* most advisers doing for the 1 to 1.75 percent annual fee they charge you? Most of the time, it's not worth paying more money for an understaffed firm to hire a middleman when you can find a more capable financial advising team that will handle all of your financial affairs in-house.

The Government's Got Your Back

Well, sort of. The government won't protect you from hidden fees, but it does (somewhat) ensure that you know they exist. Many organizations like Vanguard have calculators you can use to calculate and compare the fees you are paying. The Vanguard website says:

"You can't control the markets or a fund's performance, but you *can* control what you pay to invest. Controlling costs is smart, because costs reduce your net investment returns.

"Use this tool to compare two funds, see how their costs could erode returns, and find out how much more the higher-cost fund would have to return to outperform the lower-cost fund.

"Before investing, always consider whether a fund is appropriate for your financial goals and understand its investment objectives, strategies, and risks. You should also check the reputation of the investment adviser and learn what account services are available for the fund." [54]

There are two important takeaways. First, returns are the bottom line. With any investment, we're looking to earn high returns and maintain low risk. That leads some investors to wrongly conclude fees are irrelevant when an investment vehicle posts sizable returns. "If a fund has satisfactory returns," we might reason, "why does it matter that fees are a bit higher than usual?" That logic is sound in theory, but it fails in application. Dozens of studies have been conducted on mutual fund performance, and

---

[54] Vanguard. 2019. "Compare Fund Costs."
https://personal.vanguard.com/us/funds/tools/costcompare

they always corroborate a time-proven truth: higher-than-average expenses suggest lower-than-average performance. The contrapositive is also true: higher-than-average performance probably indicates lower-than-average expenses.

Morningstar, a company that makes its bread and butter by ranking mutual funds, concluded the same simple truth: cost is the most important factor in determining a mutual fund's quality. After examining fund data over many years, Morningstar found "mutual fund fees can sometimes be a reliable predictor of future returns, as lower-cost mutual funds generally outperform their more-expensive peers." It may seem too obvious and basic to be true, but in comparing any two mutual funds, the cheaper option will almost always make more money in the long run.[55]

Keep an Eye out for What's Hard to See

April 24, 1912. The frigid waters of the North Atlantic Ocean were calm as the ocean liner crept along. The sailing was smooth, and life was good. Little did passengers aboard the RMS Titanic know about what lay waiting.

At 11:40 p.m., a panicked warning rang out: "Iceberg right ahead!" The lookout's voice was shrill and frantic as he identified the looming hazard. The visible iceberg was underwhelming, but its danger lurked beneath the ocean's surface. Hidden from view was a mound of ice that outweighed the Titanic by ten times. Within minutes, the formidable mountain of frozen water had gutted the Titanic's hull. By three in the morning, the ship was wrenched in two. Its halves sank into the icy depths and settled along the bottom of a trench two miles deep. Fifteen-hundred passengers perished in the wreckage.

---

[55] Patty Oey. Morningstar. May 11, 2018. "Fund Fee Study: Investors Saved More than $4 Billion in 2017."
https://www.morningstar.com/blog/2018/05/11/fund-fee-study.html

Indeed, the Titanic's engineers had prepared for nearly every eventuality. The ship could withstand the mightiest ocean storms. But the ship was not equipped for dangers beneath the water's surface that the captain couldn't see.

HIDDEN FEES

Like the iceberg beneath the water's surface, hidden fees and concealed charges can pose a serious threat to our investment portfolios. We have a distinct advantage over the Titanic's captain, however. The iceberg that wrecked his ship was unmarked on nautical charts. Hidden fees, on the other hand, are always published somewhere in the fine print. Finding and understanding the fee disclosures can be difficult, but a diligent investor can overcome the odds. With a little effort and some help from an experienced second set of eyes, you may be able to adjust your portfolio to reduce or eliminate fees.

Unfortunately, hidden fees aren't the only thing that threaten to eat into our returns. If we're not careful, taxes can consume huge chunks of our retirement income. Of course, we're required to pay taxes by law. But could it be that we're paying more in taxes than the government requires? The next chapter will answer that question and more.[56]

---

[56] Quantitative Brokers. May 31, 2018. "Iceberg Right Ahead!"
https://quantitativebrokers.com/2018/05/31/iceberg-right-ahead/

CHAPTER SIX

Check Your Fuel Levels

Have you ever run out of gas in your car? It's a real nuisance, right? Most of the time, though, that's all it is: an inconvenience, but not a disaster. In a plane, it's a different story.

If a plane runs out of fuel, the results can be catastrophic. You'd think pilots and airlines would be careful to ensure a plane has enough fuel to reach its destination. In most cases, they are. But, surprisingly, planes still run out of fuel quite often. In fact, it's the sixth leading cause of aviation incidents annually.

The National Transportation Safety Board (NTSB) conducted a study in 2017 to investigate the prevalence of fuel management issues in flying. They published their findings as a public safety alert entitled "Flying on Empty." Their discoveries are staggering. Every year, about fifty planes crash because they run out of gas. And it's not that equipment fails, or that fuel doesn't make it to the engine. Ninety-five percent of the accidents were due to pilot error: failure to start the journey with enough fuel.

The statistic isn't limited to "newbies" either. Only 2 percent of incidents occurred with a student pilot at the helm. The other 98 percent had licensed pilots in control. Many of them were commercial pilots. It seems like negligence or complacency rather than inexperience is the biggest cause of fuel-related problems.

In response to this surge of avoidable plane crashes, the NTSB safety alert recommended several preemptive measures. First, you must know how much fuel you need to reach your destination. You must always know how much fuel you have onboard. And then, you must have a *fuel reserve* for each flight. Often, this reserve is needed in times of inclement weather, for holding pattern requirements, and other unforeseen encounters once airborne.[57]

In retirement planning, we likewise need a reserve—extra funds that serve as a buffer to protect us in the event of unexpected expenses. Surprises might come up that strain our retirement income if we haven't prepared. Often, those unforeseen hurdles come as taxes.

The Tax Problem

The Social Security Act was signed into effect on August 14, 1935. President Franklin D. Roosevelt was the program's originator. Social Security was just one branch of FDR's larger "New Deal" plan to boost the nation's economy and morale during the Great Depression. It was designed to combat unemployment among the working classes and to provide supplemental income for those in retirement. Roosevelt said the program was for "young people [who may] wonder what [their lot would be] when they came to old age."[58]

Legend has it that Roosevelt made another claim regarding the Social Security Act. The "New Deal" was a *big* deal, and reporters swarmed the Oval Office to capture the momentous event. Supposedly, they asked Roosevelt if Social Security benefits would

[57] National Transportation Safety Board. August 2017. "Flying on Empty." https://ntsb.gov/safety/safety-alerts/Documents/SA-067.pdf
[58] History.com. February 27, 2019. "FDR Signs Social Security Act." https://www.history.com/this-day-in-history/fdr-signs-social-security-act

be taxed. That apparently enraged the president; he slammed his fist on the desk and vowed never to tax unemployed and retired Americans. The Social Security Administration maintains that Roosevelt did no such thing, but the legend endures. Regardless, Social Security did remain tax-free during his presidency and lifetime. Unfortunately, later politicians were less keen on sacrificing a potential revenue source for the federal government.

In 1983, President Ronald Reagan instituted Social Security amendments that allowed for up to 50 percent of one's benefits to be taxed. Ten years later, President Bill Clinton increased the taxable percentage to 85. What's surprising is a retiree's annual income only needed to exceed $34,000 to have his or her benefits so heavily taxed.

It's not hard to imagine, then, that many investors discover only upon retirement that their retirement nest egg might be severely taxed. Many realize too late that they're in a higher tax bracket than expected. Some don't know that they'll need to pay taxes at all. And Social Security is just the tip of the iceberg. Many retirement investment vehicles are subject to taxation. It can all feel overwhelming. Many thus resign themselves to their over-taxed fate. After all, taxes are the law, what's the use in fighting?

Tax Evasion Versus Tax Avoidance

Taxes are the law, that's true. I'm not encouraging you to evade your taxes. When I first became a financial adviser, my father-in-law told me a joke. It goes like this: "What's the difference between tax evasion and tax avoidance?"

"Ten to twenty years."

I know, it's a little corny, but the point is sound. Investors should never withhold taxes owed to the government. But neither should they pay *more* than what they legally owe. In fact, the United States government has published a document that includes *thousands* of ways to avoid overpaying on your taxes. That's great! Right? Well, it would be great if it wasn't buried in the four-million-word, 74,608-page Internal Revenue Service Tax Code.

In case those figures are not impressive enough, let's compare the IRS tax code to some better-known works of literature. Remember Leo Tolstoy's *War and Peace*, that formidable instrument of high school torture? That one clocks in at a meager 587,287 words—just a little over 1,200 pages. Almost twice that length is J.K. Rowling's popular Harry Potter series, if we put all the books together. The Authorized King James Bible sits somewhere in the middle with 783,137 words. All three works together just barely exceed half the IRS tax code's length. It's probably not unreasonable to say the average investor will never read the government's official tax code.

Even if you were to sit down and power through the document, you'd be hard pressed to extract tax-saving tips in a comprehensive, and more importantly, practical way. You won't find convenient subheadings like, "How to Avoid Over-Taxation," or "Read This for the Bottom Line." Finding useful support in the millions of words is more akin to a treasure hunt, and you haven't been given the map.

The Internal Revenue Service itself admits the tax code is too complicated. In 1913, the document was 400 pages long. In 1939, it jumped to 504. Then things started to go terribly wrong. By 1969 it had increased to 16,500 pages, 26,300 pages by 1984, 60,044 in 2004, and finally the 74,608 we've had since 2014.[59] How could they possibly have had so much to add? In 2008, the Taxpayer Advocate Service's Annual Report to Congress from the IRS read in part: "The most serious problem facing taxpayers is the

---

[59] Kelly Phillips Erb. *Forbes.* January 10, 2013. "Tax Code Hits Nearly 4 Million Words, Taxpayer Advocate Calls It Too Complicated."
https://www.forbes.com/sites/kellyphillipserb/2013/01/10/tax-code-hits-nearly-4-million-words-taxpayer-advocate-calls-it-too-complicated/#5335ecd96e24

complexity of the Internal Revenue Code." Understatement of the year. And it didn't stop the IRS from adding another 14,564 pages six years later.

PAGES IN TAX CODE OVER TIME

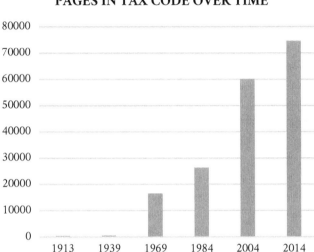

The Basics of Tax Reduction

Even without understanding the ins and outs of the IRS Tax Code, some basic rules of thumb can tremendously reduce the amount of taxes you owe Uncle Sam. Most people will draw from a combination of various accounts to fund their retirement income. Your taxes will depend heavily on *how* you withdraw your money.

It's commonly recommended that retirees fund their retirement in a certain order of withdrawals. They should begin retirement pulling money (1) from taxable accounts. When those are expended, (2) start drawing from tax-deferred retirement accounts like IRAs and 401(k)s. Finally, they should (3) tap into accounts where taxes have already been paid. The most famous of those options is the Roth IRA.

For some retirees this "withdrawal protocol" is the best course of action. But beware, one size *does not fit all,* and these times represent a different tax environment than previous decades. For example, you might have most of your savings in a 401(k) or a traditional IRA. Let's say you reach the required minimal distribution (RMD) zone. If you've accumulated a hefty sum in your 401(k), the RMD could be enough to catapult you into a higher tax bracket (even if it doesn't at first, wait until you're in your eighties when RMDs increase with decreased remaining life expectancy). Suddenly, you're facing unexpectedly high taxes. To avoid those, it may be wise to adjust your withdrawal strategy. You could move some money from your 401(k) to a more tax-friendly account or use tax-deferred accounts as your first source of retirement income.

The example above is specific and may not describe your situation. The point is that every soon-to-be retiree needs to examine his or her circumstances individually. Every soon-to-be retiree must examine his or her current tax bracket environment relative to historical rates and current economic data. Taxes are likely to rise in the future and tax strategies must account for that. It's also important to understand how retirement income is taxed in the first place. It comes down to the source. The following is not an exhaustive look at income sources and their tax set-ups, but it covers many of the most common options. I recommend always consulting a professional for an in-depth look at your specific situation, one with an expertise in tax planning. Taxes make up a critical component of any retirement plan. If your financial adviser cannot assist with tax planning, you will miss a huge slice of the retirement planning pie.

- **Tax-deferred accounts, including 401(k)s, 403(b)s, 457s, Thrift Savings Plans (TSPs), traditional IRAs, and deferred**

annuities are taxed as ordinary income upon withdrawal. Interest on certificates of deposit (CDs), savings accounts, and money market accounts are likewise considered regular income when withdrawn from tax-deferred accounts.

• **Interest received from municipal bonds is exempt from federal income tax.** *However,* you must remember that municipal bonds may be subject to state and local taxes. Make sure you know what your state expects from you before pulling income from bonds. In Arizona, where I live, interest on municipal bonds is not subject to state tax. However, municipal bond interest *is* counted toward your provisional income. That means bond interest can put you over the threshold for paying tax on your Social Security.

• **Profit from selling stocks, bonds, or mutual funds is taxed as capital gains.** That means the tax rate varies based on when you purchased the investment and how long you owned it. In general, it's best for the retiree to keep these investments for some time before selling. After a year, assets are taxed at long-term capital gains rates, which are generally more favorable than the alternative; short-term capital gains are taxed as ordinary income.

• **If you have a Roth IRA, if you're older than fifty-nine-and-one-half, and if you've owned the Roth IRA for at least five years, the money in that account is generally safe from the tax man.** As a bonus, you're not required to withdraw a required minimum distribution at age seventy-two. There's a lot more to Roth IRAs, so we'll look at them again later. If you want to skip ahead to that section, drop down a few subheadings.

• **If you have a pension, congratulations.** You're one of few who still do. Typically, pensions are taxed as regular income, but that's not always the case. For example, if you made after-tax contributions to your pension, it will probably be taxed differently. The only way to be sure is to examine your pension plan specifically.

• **Annuities are a popular retirement income source, and there are several annuity types and tax setups**. The rules depend on the annuity you own and the source of the purchase funds. As with pension plans, it's best to look at your specific annuity to see how it will be taxed. In general, however, annuities are divided into two tax groups: The part that represents a return of the principal is tax-free, and the portion representing growth is taxed as ordinary income.

• **Social Security may be taxed, depending on income**. I said that earlier, but it can't be mentioned too often. If you make "too much" money, your Social Security will be taxed. Too many retirees are shocked to find their Social Security benefits are subject to taxation. Fortunately, it's almost always possible to reduce Social Security taxes. We'll examine that a bit later.

To reiterate, this is not an exhaustive list of retirement income tax schema. It's impossible to discuss every scenario here. But hopefully it's clear that, with a little forethought and planning, it's possible to reduce taxes. Taxes will always be there, but they shouldn't be a burden in retired life. Often, a proactive approach can greatly reduce your lifetime tax obligation.

The Tax Game is a Long Game

If you're approaching retirement, or if you've already retired, you've probably been advised to capitalize on the benefits of tax-deferred accounts like 401(k)s, 403(b)s, 457s, IRAs, and TSPs. After all, that's where most people have stored their retirement savings. Tax planning is arguably *the* most important component of a retirement plan. You stand to sacrifice a lot of money if you don't prepare for taxes on your investment portfolio.

Many financial advisers preach deferment. "Defer, defer, defer," they say, "delay taxes until you absolutely *must* pay them." Their logic appears sound. Presumably, the longer you delay taxes, the lower they will eventually be. During your working years, your savings is free to compound without being reduced by taxes. And, if you happen to fall into a lower tax bracket after retirement, you will pay less in taxes than if you'd paid them when you still worked. At least, that's how it may have been in decades past.

Investors and soon-to-be retirees *must* realize that we are living in a unique economic climate and it comes with a time stamp. Taxes are as low today as they will probably ever be. On January 1, 2018, President Donald Trump's tax reform plan went into effect. It constituted the biggest change in tax law over the past three decades, and it has staggering implications for retirees and all investors alike. For one thing, the tax brackets and tax rates have been adjusted to the taxpayers' benefit. Also, the standard deduction for each tax bracket was sizably increased. For a quick comparison, check the charts that follow this section—the rates in effect for 2018 through 2025, as well as a comparison between the 2017 and 2018 standard deductions.

If you don't think that taxes stand to increase by very much, consider the historical precedent. For the better part of the twentieth century, the highest tax bracket was never lower than 70 percent. Following World War II and only ending in 1963, the highest tax bracket was a staggering 91 percent! Right now, it's only 37 percent. That leaves a lot of room for upward movement.[60]

At some point, money in tax-deferred accounts will have to be paid. Taxes are likely to increase again in 2026. For many investors, that means it may be smart to pay taxes *now* while they're still inexpensive. There are, in fact, many reasons why deferment may not be the best course of action. But, it's impossible to say what's best for you without a complete evaluation of your

---

[60] Tax Foundation. October 17, 2013. "U.S. Federal Individual Income Tax Rates History, 1862-2013 (Nominal and Inflation-Adjusted Brackets)."
https://taxfoundation.org/us-federal-individual-income-tax-rates-history-1913-2013-nominal-and-inflation-adjusted-brackets/

individual circumstances. One thing is certain, though: Taxes are lower now than they may ever be again. Act now to ensure you don't pay more in taxes than you owe.[61, 62]

2018 – 2025 TAX BRACKETS

Single Filers	Married Filing Jointly	Tax Rate
$0 – $9,525	$0 – $19,050	10%
$9,526 – $38,700	$19,051 – $77,400	12%
$38,701 – $82,500	$77,401 – $165,000	22%
$82,501 – $157,500	$165,001 – $315,000	24%
$157,501 – $200,000	$315,001 – $400,000	32%
$200,001 – $500,000	$400,001 – $600,000	35%
$500,001+	$600,001+	37%

TAX YEAR 2017 STANDARD DEDUCTIONS

Single Filers	Married Filing Jointly
$6,350	$12,700

TAX YEAR 2018 (TAX CUTS AND JOBS ACT OF 2017) STANDARD DEDUCTIONS

Single Filers	Married Filing Jointly
$12,000	$24,000

---

[61] Amelia Josephson. SmartAsset. January 12, 2019. "Here's How the Trump Tax Plan Could Affect You."
https://smartasset.com/taxes/heres-how-the-trump-tax-plan-could-affect-you
[62] Amir El-Sibaie. Tax Foundation. January 2018. "2018 Tax Brackets (Updated)."
https://files.taxfoundation.org/20180207142513/TaxFoundation-FF567-Updated.pdf

Taxes on . . . Social Security

As of this book's writing, retirees filing taxes as single individuals are subject to taxation on 85 percent of their Social Security benefits if their provisional income is more than $34,000. Couples are taxed similarly if they earn at least $44,000. As you might imagine, that would come as a shock if a retiree expects his or her Social Security to go completely untaxed.

The key to reducing Social Security taxes is in understanding the IRS' definition of taxable income. Then it's a game of Mancala, moving your money around to avoid sitting in a higher tax bracket than necessary. In some cases, wise money management can even eliminate Social Security taxes. It all comes down to your *provisional income.*

Provisional income is what the IRS uses to determine taxes on your Social Security benefits. It consists of your total gross income (excluding Social Security), tax-free interest you receive (this could be from municipal bonds, for example), and half of your Social Security benefits. If a married couple each receives $2,500 a month in Social Security benefits, right off the bat they start with $30,000 of provisional income annually. That's before additional income from part-time wages, pensions, capital gains, IRA distributions, or anything else.

Let's say for the sake of illustration that, in retirement, you earn $30,000 in returns on investments. That's your gross income. You also make $2,000 in interest on municipal bonds. Finally, you receive $24,000 from Social Security. Adding that all up (and remembering only to include *half* the Social Security benefit) gives you $44,000 in provisional income. A quick look at the table that follows shows your Social Security is probably subject to taxation on up to 85 percent! What can you do to minimize those taxes?

Lower your income.

You probably just laughed for a minute before reading on. I understand, it sounds ridiculous. "Lower my income? What kind of advice is that?!" But the trick is to lower *reportable* income without reducing any of the funds at your disposal. To do that, we need to adjust how your income is calculated.

Remember, provisional income (or taxable income) is the sum of your gross income, tax-free interest, plus half of Social Security benefits. *That's it.* Anything else falls outside the realm of IRS domain. So, while stock market gains are lumped in with provisional income, earnings inside things like annuities, which are tax-deferred, are not. Even if you reinvest stock market earnings, they must be reported as income and you must pay taxes on them. Instead, it may be prudent to move investment returns from a taxable category into one that is "tax-favored." That could mean tax-deferred or something like a Roth IRA. The business of moving money around various instruments with different tax qualities can get messy if you don't know what you're doing, and you never want to compromise potential future earnings just to save a little in taxes now. It's best to consult with a qualified financial adviser or Certified Public Accountant (CPA) before making such significant changes to your retirement portfolio.

Retirees often get confused by the variety of income sources. Social Security, IRAs, 401(k)s, stock market gains—it can feel overwhelming. To maximize our resources and minimize our taxes, each part of our retirement portfolio should constitute a cog in the greater machine. When it comes to retirement income, it's best to think of it as just that: *one* income. Sure, it's funded by several investment assets, but everything ought to work together harmoniously to provide you with the most money possible. That's the bottom line. [63]

---

[63] Social Security Administration. 2019. "Benefits Planner | Income Taxes and Your Social Security Benefit."

SOCIAL SECURITY TAXATION

Filing Status as of 2019	Provisional Income	SS Amount Subject to Tax
Married filing jointly	Under $32,000 $32,000 - $44,000 Over $44,000	0 50% 85%
Single, head of household, qualifying widow(er), married filing separately and living separately	Under $25,000 $25,000 - $34,000 Over $34,000	0 50% 85%
Married filing separately and living with spouse	Over 0	85%

Roth IRAs: Are They Worth It?

The Roth IRA was introduced in 1997. Its structure was conceived by Delaware Senator William Roth. His legacy is preserved in the eponymous retirement account that has become wildly popular in the twenty-plus years since its inception.

Senator Roth's idea was simple. He wanted to make a retirement account that was tax-free and had compounded savings. Of course, "tax-free" is never exactly tax-free. It's just a matter of *when* you pay taxes. With a Roth IRA, you pay taxes going in, but subsequent gains and withdrawals are never taxed. That makes for a pretty obvious tradeoff between the Roth IRA and traditional IRAs. Do you want to pay taxes now or in the future, presumably after retirement?

As with any investment, Roth IRAs are better suited for some investors than others. But they have some striking advantages and

https://www.ssa.gov/planners/taxes.html

benefits. Since you'll pay taxes at the onset, you have the safety of a working income to cover those expenses. You also might avoid future increases in the income tax rate. Hypothetically, if tax rates and investment returns stayed constant, a Roth IRA and traditional IRA would be identical to the penny. The only difference would be *when* you pay your taxes. But we don't live in a world with consistent investment returns and static tax rates. As I mentioned earlier, the current tax rates are lower than they may ever be again. That means there's a good chance you'll sit in a higher tax bracket after retirement. You may pay less in taxes now with a Roth IRA than if you chose to defer them. Roth IRAs can also simplify your retirement plan. Retirement comes with many variables, but a Roth IRA converts one variable (future taxes on a traditional IRA) into a known value (the tax you pay right now with a Roth).

Roth IRAs come with other benefits, too. There are no RMDs in your lifetime. The same can't be said for other accounts like IRAs and 401(k)s. Since you don't have to start withdrawing money, you're afforded more time to let the investment grow with compounded interest. Hopefully you're not late to the investment game, but if you're a few years behind, this can be a nice way to make up for lost time.

If you don't need the money in your Roth IRA, let it sit and develop. Say you retire at seventy with $500,000 in a Roth IRA. At 6 percent interest, it would grow to $1.2 million by the time you turn eighty-five! If you still don't need that money, leave it to your heirs; it remains tax-free at inheritance. However, the inheritor cannot let the money compound tax-free indefinitely. They are subject to minimum distributions that depend on their age. It's also important to consider what tax bracket your heirs will fall into. If your heirs are in a higher tax bracket, a Roth may provide tax savings for them after your death. Not so with a traditional IRA—without careful planning, the inheritance you prepared for your children or beneficiaries could be slashed and eaten up by severe taxes, especially if your inheritors collect after the current tax law expires in 2025. If you take time now to plan for such eventualities, it will curtail stress later.

Another feature of Roth IRAs: they allow you to contribute money as long as you have earned income. Age is irrelevant. If you love what you do and plan to keep working, even after having reached retirement age, this benefit may be especially appealing. But for most retirees, Roth contributions will be less impactful than Roth conversions. A conversion strategy does not require earned income and it carries no limits on the annual amounts converted from traditional IRAs to Roth IRAs. But, as I mentioned before, converting IRAs requires an expertise in taxes and broad retirement planning that the average investor does not have. I don't advise anyone to initiate Roth conversions without careful examination and guidance from a qualified financial adviser.

Investopedia explains, "Your Roth account can double as a second emergency savings account." It's true, because you can withdraw your contributions at any time for any reason. There are some provisions on when and how much of the gains you can withdraw, though. Still, that's a sizable fund at your disposal. If you've contributed $5,000 a year over twenty years, you have $100,000 in liquid money available. Gains can be withdrawn early as well, but only with good reason. Those might include buying your first home or paying for education expenses.[64]

In general, Roth IRAs can be a valuable addition to one's retirement portfolio, but they're not for everyone. If you already have a traditional IRA, you should think carefully about whether

---

[64] Amy Fontinelle. Investopedia. May 14, 2019. "How to Use Your Roth IRA as an Emergency Fund."
https://www.investopedia.com/articles/personal-finance/040714/how-use-your-roth-ira-emergency-fund.asp

it's worth converting all or a portion to a Roth. There are advantages and disadvantages to any investment opportunity and the decision should be given careful deliberation. Every investor's situation is unique. But just about every investor stands to improve the efficiency of his or her portfolio and reduce unnecessary taxes.

CHAPTER SEVEN

Flying with Your Flaps Down – Avoid the Drag of Debt

Frank McNamara didn't know he was changing the world one fateful day in 1949. As the story goes, McNamara was at dinner with his wife and several clients at New York City's ritzy Major Cabins Grill. As the dinner wound down, McNamara reached for his wallet to cover the tab, only to realize that had forgotten it. His wife had to pay for dinner—something that in 1949 America humiliated Frank. From the angst of his embarrassment, Mr. McNamara conceived an idea that would change the course of history: a multipurpose charge card, sort of an officially recognized "IOU." The idea caught on quickly among the elite restaurants of Manhattan, and McNamara called his new charge card company "Diners Club."

Diners Club wasn't the first attempt at a credit card. In the 1920s, department stores and oil companies offered trusted clients the option to pay with a metal "charge plate," or "courtesy card," and settle their tabs later. They operated like modern day store cards; solely the issuing company accepted the card. But the idea didn't catch on until Diners Club was founded, and the breadth of McNamara's idea was unique.

"Someday," McNamara said, "restaurants all over New York will honor this card." If he only knew how understated that estimation would prove to be. By the end of 1950, Diners Club had 20,000 members. That number more than doubled to 42,000 by 1951. In 1953, Diners Club received international recognition, and by 1958, it was just one of several major companies issuing credit cards, including American Express.[65]

In the seventy-plus years since Diners Club's inception, credit cards have revolutionized the way Americans consume. It has also perpetuated a nationwide debt problem. In October 2018, credit card debt in the United States totaled $1.037 trillion. And yet, that's just the tip of the iceberg. Consumer debt in its entirety totaled $3.964 trillion in that same month. The majority is comprised of education and auto loans, $1.564 trillion and $1.143 trillion, respectively.

Consumer debt can cripple the individual spender. It includes revolving debt (credit cards), and fixed-payment loans, both of which put a tremendous strain on one's investment capacity. Consumer debt is especially devastating when the economy goes into a recession. If we lose our job, we risk going into default. In turn, our credit scores plummet and we lose the ability to take out loans in the future. A vicious cycle ensues. On top of it all, unexpected medical bills and other essential expenses can force us into debt we weren't expecting.[66]

I probably don't need to tell you how distressing debt can be. At some point in our lives, most of us contend with debt to some

[65] Claire Tsosie. NerdWallet. February 9, 2017. "The History of the Credit Card."
https://www.nerdwallet.com/blog/credit-cards/history-credit-card/
[66] Kimberly Amadeo. The Balance. May 14, 2019. "Consumer Debt Statistics, Causes and Impact."
https://www.thebalance.com/consumer-debt-statistics-causes-and-impact-3305704

degree or another. Many of us remember the Great Recession of 2008 and the tech bubble burst of the early 2000s. It can take years to recover from heavy debt. Many of us do everything within our power to stay debt-free. But let me tell you a little secret: good investors are almost always in debt.

Now before you run off to max out your credit cards because a financial adviser said that good investors carry debt, allow me to explain what I mean. I'm talking about *good debt*, and it's easy to miss the difference.

Good Debt Versus Bad Debt

In short, good debt helps generate income and increases your net worth, even if not right away. It embodies the adage, "it takes money to make money." Bad debt is everything else.

Unfortunately, the distinction between good and bad is not always so easy to identify. Some things lie within a gray area. It would take an exhaustive study to categorize all types of debt as good or bad, and to what degree. But here is a brief examination of the most common forms of debt.

The Good

1. Education. For a recent graduate, a student loan might feel like anything but good debt. But it can be. In the long run, a college education can make a world of difference. It increases one's earning potential and improves one's chances of finding good employment. Student debt normally pays for itself after a few years in the workforce and by the time retirement rolls around, college educated investors will have probably earned a return on investment amounting to hundreds of thousands of dollars or more. Still, the way you (or your children) pay for college should be strategized in advance. There are too many teenagers making major life decisions with little understanding of the financial repercussions. If school put you into six figures of debt, there was probably a less expensive way to fund your education.

2. Business Ownership. A business is expensive to start. Many new companies don't turn a profit until years after operation begins. That doesn't necessarily mean its owner will not make money, however. It took the dot-com giant Amazon years to turn a profit, and fourteen years to make cumulatively as much as the company earned in just a single quarter of 2018. Despite that slow growth, Amazon's owner, Jeff Bezos, has long been a billionaire. The whole point of business is to make money, and if it's well managed, a business will return handsomely on initial investments. Besides monetary gain, owning your own business often yields intangible benefits like independence from third-party management and the opportunity to do something you love. Starting a business can be risky, and if it fails, your initial investment is lost, sending this category straight to the "bad debt" column.[67]

3. Investing. General investment is itself a type of debt. It's the most obvious example of good debt. An investor sacrifices some money in the present to earn more money in the future. It's straightforward. Of course, money must be invested wisely for it to yield positive returns. Bonds are especially "good" debt. The bond market is over twice as large as the stock market and bonds are simple debt. You lend money to entities like the federal government, corporations, and municipalities. Eventually you're repaid with interest. At the moment, however, with interest rates near all-time lows, bonds may not provide the highest expected returns, however certain types tend to be relatively low risk.

---

[67] Alison Griswold and Jason Karain. *Quartz.* February 1, 2018. "It Took Amazon 14 Years to Make as Much in Net Profit as It Did Last Quarter." https://qz.com/1196256/it-took-amazon-amzn-14-years-to-make-as-much-net-profit-as-it-did-in-the-fourth-quarter-of-2017/

The Bad

1. Credit Cards. Here's one that teeters the line. On one hand, credit is essential in today's economy and credit cards often come with rewards like flight miles, cash back, and dining points that add value to every purchase. But keeping a balance on a credit card is a different story. Credit card interest rates are exorbitant, sometimes as high as almost 30 percent, and that interest earns nothing in the way of equity. Interest paid on credit cards is money lost. It's best never to leave a balance.

2. General Consumer Goods. Buying clothes, fast food, groceries, gasoline, vacations, and the like with borrowed money from personal loans is a bad idea. Most consumer goods have little intrinsic value. Take clothes, for example. Have you ever been to a thrift store? Even well-preserved clothes sell at a fraction of their retail value. We buy consumer goods out of necessity, but we never expect to earn money from them. To pay interest on a loan to buy valueless things is financially irresponsible.

3. Automobiles. Cars could also fall into a gray area. They fulfill an essential purpose in modern life. Strictly speaking, however, vehicles don't make us money. That makes them a form of bad debt. If you were to buy a new car, drive off the lot, turn around, and sell your car back to the dealership, you'd lose a significant amount of money. It's just the way it works; most cars depreciate immediately, and their value never comes back up. A good rule of thumb is to purchase a vehicle you can actually afford and pay for it in cash.

Good Debt 2.0: A Home Mortgage

You may have noticed real estate is missing from both of the preceding lists. That's because it deserves a category of its own. A mortgage is necessary debt, as most investors know. But unlike most debt, good or bad, *most investors should not pay off a mortgage as quickly as possible.*

That surprises many investors. Since the mortgage was invented, homeowners have been eager to pay off their debt quickly. It's advice that's been passed down from generation to generation. As with most modern-day investment, though, we can't follow the example of our parents and grandparents. What worked in the past may not work today, or worse, it could be to our financial detriment.

In the 1920s, before the Great Depression, mortgages were five- or ten-year loans for half the value of a house and property. They were known as "callable loans." Banks retained the right to demand at any time that homeowners pay off the balance of their mortgage loan. Families that failed to pay off their loan were subject to foreclosure and displacement. With foreclosure an ever-looming threat, common practice was to pay off mortgage debt as soon as possible lest the bank catch you off guard.

Then housing prices fell by 51 percent during the Great Depression. Banks started calling in mortgage balances and homeowners couldn't afford to pay them. By 1935, 10 percent of all homes in the United States were in foreclosure.[68]

To quell the disaster, President Roosevelt instituted several housing laws—another facet of his New Deal. The Home Owners' Loan Corporation bought a million defaulted mortgages from U.S. banks and reinstituted them. They were not the same five-year callable loans, however. Instead, the reissued loans were changed to long-term fixed rate mortgages—the same that we know today. The Federal Housing Administration started mortgage insurance. A secondary market was created that made

---

[68] UC Davis Graduate School of Management. January 10, 2010. "Real Estate Bubble Crystal Ball? The Great Depression and Manhattan Home Prices."
https://gsm.ucdavis.edu/research/real-estate-bubble-crystal-ball-great-depression-and-manhattan-home-prices

mortgages more accessible. The Federal Deposit Insurance Corporation insured bank deposits. And the Glass-Steagall Act separated investment banks from retail banks, forbidding the former to invest deposited funds in risky investment ventures like the stock market.[69]

While these changes were designed to halt an imploding economy, they changed the way mortgage lenders operate in the United States. Mortgages became easier for homeowners to procure and safer for banks to lend. Later government amendments would similarly improve the accessibility of housing loans and encourage home ownership.

But still, it would seem logical to pay off a mortgage early. If you buy a $500,000 house with a thirty-year fixed mortgage at 4 percent interest with a 20 percent down payment, the interest over three decades could be close to $300,000. Your $500,000 house has effectively turned into a $800,000 house. If you can afford to make some payments early, you might undercut the interest and save hundreds of thousands of dollars. It's a no-brainer, right?

Wrong.

It all comes down to the time value of money.

The time value of money (or TVM) is a financial concept which says money available for investment *now* is worth more than the same sum of money in the future because it has a higher potential earning capacity. The potential earning capacity is based on compound interest; that means interest is calculated based on the principle investment *and* accumulated interest.

Besides sacrificing millions of dollars in potential earning capacity, paying extra in mortgage payments gives up cash

---

[69] Kimberly Amadeo. *The Balance.* June 27, 2018. "What are Mortgages? Their Types, History, and Impact on the Economy."
https://www.thebalance.com/what-is-a-mortgage-types-history-impact-3305946

liquidity. Once money is applied to a home, it's difficult to get back quickly. For example, let's say you have $100,000 in cash and you decide to buy a $300,000 house. By the way, you're in the 25 percent tax bracket (for simplicity of numbers, I'm using a pre-Trump tax law bracket). You decide you want to pay off your mortgage as quickly as possible. You take out a fifteen-year loan at 3.5 percent interest. To further offset your mortgage, you put your entire $100,000 toward a down payment on the house. When all is said and done, your monthly payment comes to $1,530. But now, imagine you lose your job.

What will you do? Your monthly mortgage payment of $1,530 is due, no matter what. You don't have anything in the way of savings because you contributed your entire $100,000 toward a down payment. Now it doesn't seem to matter too much that your mortgage will be paid off in fifteen years. Money is tight, but all your resources are tied up in a house and you can't get them back.

Imagine instead that you took a thirty-year mortgage at 4 percent interest and paid a $60,000 down payment. Your monthly payment comes to $1,146 and you've still got $40,000 in cash to invest. That money will earn compound interest and, if you lose your job, you will have it plus the returns on investment to support you and pay your mortgage while you find another job.[70]

As you advance in age, it gets more important that you have ready access to your assets. Losing your job is just one of many unexpected events that can beset you and demand hefty payments. If your money is housed in an interest-bearing account, you have access at any time.

There is little to be said for paying off a mortgage early. Doing so may stifle our investment potential and limit potential growth.

---

[70] Edelman Financial Services. "11 Great Reasons to Carry a Big, Long Mortgage." https://www.edelmanfinancialengines.com/education-center/articles/11-great-reasons-to-carry-a-big-long-mortgage

It can be tempting to offset what many perceive as just another major debt. But it's important to remember that some debt is good, and a mortgage sits at the top of that list.

Have you ever heard someone say, "heads I win, tails you lose?" It seems to pop up in every sitcom at some point or another—the incorrigible trickster swindles another character into doing what he or she wants with a rigged coin toss. The trickster always wins whether the coin lands on heads or tails. Mortgages are the same way; the investor always wins. If interest rates go up, you've lucked out. Keep your low-rate mortgage and earn higher interest in bonds, certificates of deposit, and other interest-bearing investments. If interest rates drop, refinance and lock in the lower rates. It's a win-win situation.

I've said it many times already, but it bears repeating: We're living in the lowest interest-rate environment since the Mayans. As rates rise in coming decades, why would anyone be in a rush to pay off historically low and locked-in interest rate mortgages?

In this section, I've identified why you shouldn't pay off your mortgage early. By way of review, following are seven reasons to carry a mortgage:

1) **Your mortgage doesn't affect your home's value**. Your home will rise or fall in value regardless of whether you have a mortgage or not. If you buy the house outright, it's a bit like having all that money stored under your mattress. Any equity in the house essentially earns no interest.

2) **A mortgage won't stop you from building equity in the house.** It's true, paying off your mortgage contributes to the growth of equity in your house. But that's not the only nor the most powerful way that equity develops. Your house is bound to grow in value over the decades that you carry a mortgage, which

contributes handsomely to the total equity in your home, as demonstrated by the following graph. [71]

Equity Buildup

$300,000 home with 30-year mortgage and $50,000 downpayment

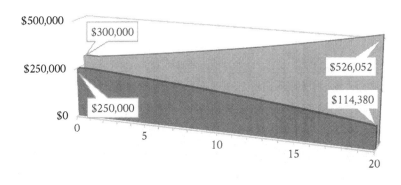

■ Mortgage Owed ■ Home Equity

3) **A mortgage is cheap money.** In other words, mortgages come with about the lowest interest you can ever expect to receive on loans of that size. Mortgages are low-risk for banks; they have your house as collateral if you fail to repay them. That allows banks to offer low interest rates.

4) **Mortgage payments get easier over time.** Anyone who's ever rented knows the pain of watching the price increase from year to year. A mortgage, on the other hand, is fixed. Eventually, the price of your monthly mortgage payment may become laughable. I met a gentleman once who bought his house in the 1950s and paid $95 a month. What's funny is it had been a challenge for him to make his payments when he first bought the

---

[71] Ibid.

place. Within a few years, however, his income had significantly outpaced his piddly mortgage.

5) **Mortgages allow you to sell without selling.** Huh? Sell without selling, what does that mean? If your house's value has increased significantly, you may want to sell and pocket the earned equity before housing values drop again. But, it's not always convenient to uproot your family and start anew. Fortunately, there's still a way to pull your home's equity—you can simply get a new mortgage! In so doing, you pocket the equity that has developed on your home—effectively "selling" your house—without having to pack up and get out. Remortgaging is not always advisable, but in some cases, it can be a savvy decision.

6) **Mortgages allow you to build more wealth.** The money you save when you don't pay off a mortgage early can be put into higher-earning investment vehicles that will make you more money in the long-term.

7) **Mortgages provide liquidity and flexibility.** A $500,000 lump sum invested in a house is $500,000 that you can't access readily when you need it. In addition to the previous point, a mortgage allows you to invest your money in liquid assets for times when you need quick access to cash.

Real Estate Investing

While we're talking about home ownership, it's worth discussing real estate investing more generally. Some investors are interested in purchasing more than just a primary residence. But for those looking to make real estate a larger part of their portfolio, buying up more houses isn't necessarily the best course of action.

Home appreciation can be misleading. Imagine you bought a house in the 1970s for less than $100,000. After twenty years, you sold the house for $450,000. That's incredible appreciation, right? Yes, but how does it compare to other investment opportunities over the same twenty-year span? If we calculate the annual rate of return on that house over twenty years of ownership, it comes to something like 9.5 percent. Now, that's not bad at all. In fact, compared to the average rate of return we can expect on most investments, 9.5 percent is outstanding. However, from the 1970s to the 1990s, all investments fared well. The Standard & Poor's 500 averaged 15.8 percent per year. A well-diversified portfolio would have done even better. Also, the appreciation on a home is often redirected toward upkeep and taxes. The cost to maintain and improve a home is huge, and that expense chips away at any appreciation in the house's value.

Now, if you'd bought that home to live in, maybe to raise a family, then a 9.5 percent annual rate of return is excellent. The house served an important function in your life and the money it made you was a secondary, welcome benefit. If, however, the house was strictly an investment opportunity, its appreciation proved underwhelming. For the investor who likes real estate, real estate investment trusts (REITs) may be a better option.

So, what's a real estate investment trust? It's a pooling of investors who collectively own a professionally managed portfolio of real estate. Each REIT owns a portfolio of properties. When you invest in a REIT, you're investing in companies that build, own, and/or manage real estate that makes money. That can include housing developments, condominiums, offices, shopping centers, malls, hospitals, and more.

The Dow Jones Wilshire REIT Index (DJ Wilshire REIT), a subset of the Wilshire U.S. Real Estate Securities Index, measures U.S. publicly traded real estate investment trusts, much like the more famous Dow Jones Industrial Average measures the performance of thirty publicly owned companies in the stock market. Over the twenty years our investor owned his house, the DJ Wilshire REIT appreciated at 15.3 percent. That far outpaced the S&P 500 and the rate of appreciation of our investor's home.

But 15.3 was an unusual rate of appreciation. REITs are not typically so productive. And when real estate plummets, like it did in 2008, REITs naturally depreciate in kind. So, are they a worthy investment vehicle? For some investors, maybe.

Paul Merriman, a financial adviser whose work has been widely cited in the investment world, is a strong proponent of real estate investment trusts. Still, he admits they have their drawbacks. For one thing, REITs are volatile. They tend to perform tremendously or dismally, and the transition can be hard to predict. That makes them a poor short-term investment technique. Everything I've said in this book has advocated for long-term investment strategies. But if you still have your heart set on short-term turnover, be warned: REITs are *not* the place to look. Their volatility means poor market-timing can sink an investment in the short term. In 2007, the DJ Wilshire REIT fell by 17.6 percent. It fell another 39.2 percent in 2008. In those two years, the DJ Wilshire REIT lost more than half its value. That was a bad time for the short-term investor.

In the long-run, however, REITs have performed well. From 1975 to 2006, REITs had an annualized return of 16.7 percent. And even including 2007 and 2008, REITs annualized return still came to 14.1 percent from 1975 to 2014. That outperformed the S&P 500 by about 2 percent over the same block of time. Their long-term growth potential makes REITs a possible investment option for a retirement portfolio.

But there's another reason to consider investing in REITs. They may reduce portfolio volatility. "Now, wait a minute," you might be thinking, "didn't you just say that REITs are often volatile?" On their own, yes, REITs can be unpredictable. But as part of a larger investment portfolio, they can add stability and balance. It all comes back to diversification.

Remember, part of diversifying a portfolio in the right way is to include investment types that perform and react *dissimilarly* from each other. Herein lies the beauty of real estate investment trusts. Historically, REITs have performed slightly better than the S&P 500, but we can't be certain that trend will continue. At best, we can be reasonably confident that REITs and the S&P 500 Index will have comparable returns in coming years. REITs should not be introduced to one's portfolio with the expectation that overall returns will improve. However, REITs occasionally move up when the stock market declines, and vice versa. In fact, REITs are often out-of-sync with other major equity asset classes. That said, some people exaggerate REITs' independence from the stock market. In reality, comparing REITs and other stocks in markets like the S&P 500 is like comparing apples and oranges.[72]

REITs may make your portfolio returns more consistent, which translates to a more stable retirement income. However, I don't typically recommend to my clients that they invest in REITs *directly*. It's not that REITs are a poor investment. However, in a broadly based, globally diversified portfolio, you will own several real estate companies and REITs within the context of the portfolio design. This means going out and buying a specific REIT index fund is creating unnecessary overlap within the portfolio (you would own the same thing in different funds). Nonetheless, REITs appeal to some investors and they've risen in popularity in recent years. It's wise for a well-rounded investor to understand the basics of how they work, at least.

---

[72] Sean Ross. Investopedia. May 20, 2015. "Has Real Estate or the Stock Market Performed Better Historically?"
https://www.investopedia.com/ask/answers/052015/which-has-performed-better-historically-stock-market-or-real-estate.asp

The Bottom Line

Investors will always contend with a measure of debt. Investment itself is fundamentally a form of debt. A key to sound financial planning is avoiding *bad debt*. Credit card balances especially can cripple your investment capacity. On the other hand, home ownership and mortgage debt are valuable to the prudent investor. Good debt allows us to use our money more effectively in developing our retirement nest egg. As you plan for your retirement, remember the time value of money and look for investment opportunities that capitalize on compound interest.

CHAPTER EIGHT

The Corrosive Danger of Inflation

I feel a little bad for picking on British European Airlines earlier, but I'm about to pick on them some more. I don't think the company will mind; BEA declared bankruptcy in 1974 and was absorbed by the airline that would later become British Airways. Maybe the following story had something to do with the company's demise.

In 1971, thirteen years after British European Airlines flight 609 crashed and killed twenty-three people, BEA flight 706 took off from Runway 28 L of London Heathrow Airport with fifty-five passengers and eight crew members. It was headed for Salzburg, Austria.

The aircraft took off at 9:34 a.m. Within a few minutes, the plane had reached cruising altitude, and all was normal. Then, at 10:09, air traffic control in Brussels received a panicked communication:

"We're going down, 706, we are going down!"

Shortly thereafter the captain declared an official state of emergency.

"Mayday, mayday!" he said over the intercom, "we're going down! Mayday, mayday, mayday, we're going down vertically!"

Screaming passengers were audible in the background. The crew desperately tried to identify the problem. They begged for saving advice, but air traffic control was helpless amidst the chaos. The pilot's voice was suddenly awash with the sound of rushing air and roaring propellers. At 10:10 a.m., the final transmission came through in garbled sound bites:

"Out of control . . . No rudder . . . Ahh, this is it!"

Then, silence.

Air Traffic Control tried several times to contact Flight 706. There was no answer. Within two minutes, a routine flight had cascaded into disaster. All sixty-three passengers and crew members died.

For a plane to go from functional to fragmented in two minutes, something extreme must have happened, right? "Up to the time of the emergency call," the official report says, "there had been no indication of any abnormality in the flight." Then, within fifty-four seconds, "both horizontal tail surfaces with their associated elevators became detached from the airframe in flight." In other words, the rear of the plane broke off. What remained swiftly entered a nosedive and crashed into Belgian farmland, exploding on impact. "The accident made a large crater in [the] grass field." Rescue services that responded to the accident described a horrific scene. One responder said that of the sixty-three people on board, "what we have found so far is barely enough to reconstitute *one* body."

The crash was dramatic. So dramatic that rumor spread of sabotage and terrorism. Some British suspected that Northern Irish extremists were to blame. Evidence proved otherwise. The plane's histrionic fragmentation was only symptomatic of an underlying issue. Later investigation revealed the crash had a subtle and insidious culprit: Corrosion.

The plane's bulkhead was in such poor condition that it likely took years of sustained corrosion to compromise the aircraft's shell as thoroughly as it was. It's not that maintenance crews were negligent in their duties. Rather, "the aircraft had been maintained in accordance with an approved maintenance schedule." But corrosion is just that treacherous. Experts found severe corrosion where the fuselage met the rear pressure bulkhead. The deterioration extended "from the front face [of the metal] through the sheet." Although extensive, the damage was undetectable by maintenance crews.[73]

Hopefully I haven't scared you off from ever flying again. Rest assured, modern maintenance protocols are infinitely better than they were in 1971. Immediately following the Flight 706 catastrophe, BEA and other airlines introduced a special inspection technique designed to catch corrosion before it compromises flight safety.

Metal corrosion eats away at the surface. Similarly, inflation corrodes wealth. It can take several years, but when the damage manifests itself, it does so in a big way. Inflation chips away at the value of money, and if we're not careful, we might not notice until the value of our retirement nest egg has been undermined.

Inflation and Your Retirement

Inflation is not a new problem. In fact, as we'll see later, inflation has been a defining characteristic of world economies ever since paper currency was invented. But despite its normalcy in

---

[73] Accidents Investigation Branch. 1972. "British European Airways Vanguard G—APEC. Report on the Accident which Occurred at Aarsele, Belgium on 2 October 1971." https://assets.publishing.service.gov.uk/media/5422f37ee5274a131700048f/15-1972_G-APEC.pdf

economics and financial planning, many still neglect to plan for inflation in their retirement.

In simple terms, Investopedia defines inflation as the "the rate at which the general level of prices for goods and services is rising and, consequently, the purchasing power of currency is falling." In day-to-day life, prices inflate minimally enough that it often goes unperceived. The average annual rate of inflation in the United States is about 3 percent. That means a loaf of bread which costs $1.00 today will cost $1.03 in a year—hardly breaking the bank. But that seemingly inconsequential devaluation of money is profound over time. Remember, inflation is a compounding rate of interest. If inflation sits at just above 3 percent for about twenty years, the prices of goods and services will double. Taken another way, the value of our money will have been slashed in two. Think about this. How much did you make at your first real job? How much did your first car cost? You may laugh when you think how much further your money went back then. That's the power of inflation at work.[74]

Retirement planning behooves us to ensure steady annual income for twenty to thirty years. If you need $60,000 a year today, it's not safe just to multiply that number by thirty. On the contrary, the same standard of living will presumably cost $120,000 in twenty years.

To account for inflation, it's best to update your living expenses every year. Five percent is probably a safe increase. Fortunately, you won't have to rely on your portfolio for the entirety of your retirement income. Social Security benefits will cover some, maybe a pension contributes a bit. Things like annuity payments and rental income from real estate can further subsidize your

---

[74] Cindy Collins. *Forbes*. February 28, 2018. "Will Your Retirement Income Withstand Future Inflation?"
https://www.forbes.com/sites/forbesfinancecouncil/2018/02/28/will-your-retirement-income-withstand-future-inflation/#35ee5c001433

retirement. Let's keep our example figure of $60,000 and assume that half is covered by Social Security and other income sources distinct from your retirement portfolio. That leaves $30,000 to provide yourself for your *first year* of retirement. You'll need more with each subsequent year. A quick rule of thumb says to take the figure for which your retirement portfolio is responsible in your first year of retirement and multiply it by twenty-five. The result is a rough estimate of the minimum you should have in your portfolio upon retirement. In this case, $30,000 times twenty-five yields $750,000.

Now here's the rub: that $750,000—or at least a portion of it— *must* be positioned to earn compounding interest over the course of your retirement. Earlier we talked about the 4 percent rule and its failure to meet modern day retirement needs. It fails because many who use that formula don't fully account for inflation. Withdrawal percentages will vary from year to year, but they will generally increase to meet rising living expenses. I sometimes meet retirees who feel inflation is "no big deal" because they're not "long-term investors" anymore. That's the wrong way to think. Statistics indicate a sixty-five-year-old retiree has a good chance to live another thirty years! It's not enough for your retirement plans to merely get you *to* retirement, they must also get you *through* retirement. A retirement portfolio's growth must be commensurate with the inflation rate or your money will steadily devalue, and you risk expending your retirement nest egg.

The Advent of Inflation

Inflation hasn't always been a problem. Economies existed for centuries before inflation was introduced. But those economies traded in valuable currency. See, inflation only develops when money is stripped of intrinsic value. A gold coin has genuine worth; gold is a rare and precious metal. Acquiring more gold directly increases one's wealth. Paper money, however, has only the value that we assign it, and sometimes it can lose even that.

China was the first nation to introduce paper currency. They called it *jiaozi*, and it appeared under the Song dynasty sometime between the 900s and 1100s. It still played second fiddle to metal coins, though, until the Yuan dynasty rose to power in the late 1200s.

Kublai Khan was the first emperor of the Yuan Dynasty. He assumed power in 1260. He promptly issued *zhongtong yuanbao jiaochoa* paper currency, generally shortened to *zhongtong chao*. Kublai Khan was determined to establish *zhongtong chao* as the international standard. He went about it wisely. Kublai Khan recognized the need to back paper money with a metal reserve. He chose silver. *Zhongtong chao* could be freely exchanged for silver with a slight interest fee imposed. But silver was forbidden from use in commercial transactions. That imposition lent tremendous credibility to the proliferating *zhongtong chao* and the paper money was quickly accepted into everyday life by the Chinese people. By the 1270s, paper was firmly set as the standard, from the south to the far northern frontier territories. For the first time in history, paper was the sole currency of an entire nation. The standardization even promoted political accord and the country experienced a unification that had eluded previous dynasties. Historical records report "paper monies [were] more popular than gold and silver," even among the people.

During this early stage in the use of paper money, the Yuan government was careful to monitor and regulate fluctuation in value. Besides matching paper money with silver (and some copper) reserves, the government kept storehouses of important commodities like rice and grain. If, for example, the country experienced famine and the price of rice increased, the government could introduce its own rice stores to the market, thereby reestablishing equilibrium.

In general, the young government demonstrated incredible insight and forethought in the development of its unique monetary system. Unfortunately, prudency didn't last.

Do you remember when you first learned about money—how basic exchange works? I think I was in second or third grade when I first learned rudimentary economics. It seemed straightforward to me. My teacher explained how one must earn money to exchange for goods and services. Some people have more money than others. Sadly, some people don't have enough money to buy even the things they need. "Well, that's silly," I thought. "Why doesn't the president just print more money for the people who don't have enough? Has no one thought of this before? The solution is so simple. I must be some kind of genius!"

As it turns out, the Chinese did think of that solution, and they quickly learned why it is not a solution at all. The Yuan dynasty didn't print more money to help the poor and needy, though. Typical of large and powerful governments, Yuan China's monetary needs were to fund ambitious war campaigns.

In 1276, the Yuan dynasty was fully engaged in war efforts to expand its borders. The growing military expenditures eventually exceeded the government's budget. To fund the war campaign, silver reserve money from warehouses around the country was transported to the country's capital and used for military purposes. That meant paper money was no longer matched with silver. When the military expenses increased further, the Yuan leaders made an executive decision to print more money, further depreciating the value of *zhongtong chao* and introducing widespread inflation for the first time in history. But that wasn't to be the worst of it.

To combat the inflation, the Yuan government decided to issue a new paper currency that would carry five times the value of the original *zhongtong chao*. The new currency was not backed by silver standard and it, too, quickly fell in value. As the government printed more money, it plummeted further into fiscal deficit.

By 1350, the Yuan government had reached its fifth edition of new money. Records indicate that in 1352, issuance of the new currency skyrocketed price levels to 267 times that of the Yuan dynasty when it was securely backed by silver. The prices of grained rice, silver, and copper went up by 250, 400, and 800 units respectively. Commodity prices rose by a staggering 50,000.

The economy had inflated so spectacularly that it's more accurately termed "hyperinflation." In 1356, the people had enough. They rejected paper currency. A Bible verse, Ezekiel 7:19, predicts people will throw their money into the streets. Well, it certainly came true in fourteenth-century China.[75]

Paper currency in Yuan China is a fascinating and important study. It is the first instance of inflation according to our modern definition. Furthermore, apparently China's experience with paper money preceded the Western world's experience by several hundred years. We are prepared to deal with inflation in our economy due in large part to the lessons we learned from Imperial China's ordeal.

Individually, we can't do much to combat general inflation in our economy. But we can prepare our portfolios to survive the inevitable increase in living expenses during our decades of retirement. Investors cannot get "too conservative" in retirement so their investments don't adjust as inflation rises. Imagine going to the bank and having it tell you that your savings account lost 3 percent last year. The $100,000 you had before is now worth $97,000. Would you keep your money invested there for another five years? Of course not!

---

[75] Guan Hanhui and Mao Jai. Peking University. "The Silver Standard, Warfare and Inflation: The Mechanism of Paper Money in Yuan China."
http://mx.nthu.edu.tw/~tkho/workshop/Paper3.pdf

In real life, the number in your bank account will not decrease, but the devaluing effect of that story is a real thing. With every year an investment fails to grow commensurate with inflation, its value decreases. The bank might still show $100,000, but those dollars may only have the purchasing power of last year's $97,000.

The same thing occurs in fixed income vehicles that return your principal when the bond matures. Since they don't account for inflation, the principal you invested ten or twenty years ago is worth much less when you get it back. Similarly, I see far too many retirees with income riders on annuities that do not adjust for inflation. Sure, they have lifetime income guaranteed by an insurance company, but that income will be approximately 3 percent less valuable each year as it arrives.

A sound retirement plan thus places great emphasis on combating inflation. It will likewise work to avoid over taxation, hidden fees and expenses, and burdensome debt.

This section has prepared us to overcome typical investor obstacles and pitfalls. But what will you do with your retirement plan? What does retirement mean to you? The next section will help you shape the retirement of your dreams.

Section Three:

The Final Approach

Stopping at third base adds no more to the score than striking out.
It doesn't matter how well you start if you fail to finish.

—BILLY SUNDAY

CHAPTER NINE

Finding a Middle Ground

There are many types of planes. Each is designed with a specific purpose. There are small, low-flying propeller planes for short-distance trips, regional jets to take you cross-country, big commercial aircrafts that can circumnavigate the earth, and military jets that can exceed the speed of sound. You can further distinguish plane types based on wing configuration—monoplanes, biplanes, triplanes, and quadplanes—which can be further subdivided into tandem-wing, delta-wing, swept-wing, and flying-wing crafts. Some planes are classified based on landing equipment and include floatplanes, flying boats, and amphibians. There are gliders and sail planes, typically reserved for recreational use. If you want to be inclusive of general aircraft, there are hot air balloons, blimps, and ultralights. The list of distinctions goes on and on.

Every plane was designed with a function in mind. As you might expect, most pilots select the plane most suited to their flying needs. But there is a group of pilots who fly planes contrary to their intended purpose. In fact, a whole industry exists around these pilots. It's called ferry flying.

The ferry flying industry comprises elite pilots, most of whom probably have a screw loose. Their job, in short, is to deliver planes across the ocean. They don't ship them, however; they fly them. That may seem obvious. It's much faster to fly a plane to its destination than to put it on a cargo ship. But these pilots aren't delivering Boeing 777s, not even close. More like bush planes and four-seater Cessnas.

Navigating an ocean in a plane that small poses many serious issues. The most obvious is probably fuel capacity. The shortest stretch across the Atlantic is 700 miles. These planes average 200 to 400 miles per tank of fuel. To overcome that hurdle, pilots rig makeshift surplus tanks to the planes' exteriors.

A second problem is most small aircraft are unpressurised. That makes it inadvisable to fly above 10,000 feet, lest the pilot pass out. Yet, flying at low altitude subjects the plane to extreme weather conditions that larger pressurized planes avoid by flying at 36,000 to 40,000 feet.

These conditions make for a tumultuous journey, but one that ferry fliers relish. To them, it's "real flying"—no fancy technology, no cushy cockpit—just a pilot, a plane, and the open skies. Most of these pilots have flown dozens of successful trips across the ocean in planes that were never designed for that job. But inevitably it seems, for those who stay in the business too long, disaster is unavoidable. As talented as they are, a huge percentage of pilots lose their lives on ferry flying missions. It's just too easy for things to go wrong.

The Best Odds at Retirement Success

If I had to isolate the biggest mistakes I see among soon-to-be retirees, they would be (1) not having an experienced guide, (2) not having a comprehensive retirement plan, and (3) carrying too much risk. I've talked about it earlier in this book, but it's worth emphasizing. As you approach retirement, you cannot invest like you did in years past. But "no risk, no reward," right? Well, not really. Very few people should invest exclusively in the stock market, but a young investor can get away with using most of his or her money to buy equities. Aging investors often can't do the same. Sure, the greatest opportunities for growth demand higher risk. But growth potential is not always worth high risk when you're approaching retirement. You *might* survive post-work life unscathed, but there's a chance you will damage your portfolio and compromise your retirement irreparably. Yes, some pilots can cross the Atlantic in a bush plane, but is it worth the risk for the average traveler? In the same way, you *might* survive retirement with all your money invested in the stock market, but is it worth the risk?

Some retirees choose to approach investment from the other extreme. To protect their hard-earned money, they choose the safest route possible. That includes certificates of deposit (CDs), Treasury bonds, and fixed annuities. To put their money strictly in "safe" options is a mistake for most. It's easy to eat away at your savings when you don't have a working income anymore. To ensure your retirement income lasts for the duration of your life, your money needs to make more money, at a higher rate of return than so-called "safe" options often afford on their own. That makes balancing risk the key. If you're too risky, there is a good possibility you might go broke. If you're too conservative, well, you still run the risk of going broke.

Ultimately, each investor will have individual investment needs to match his or her unique life and circumstances. It's not possible to outline a one-size-fits-all retirement plan because such a thing cannot possibly exist. If it did, there'd be no need for financial advisers. However, I hope this book has given you several financial principles to get you started on your financial journey.

Striking a Balance

The key with any portfolio is to strike the right balance with a sort of "hybrid" investment plan. What constitutes "balance" will vary from person to person. Having some stock market investments under the protective watch of a credentialed financial adviser is healthy in a retirement portfolio. Certificates of deposit and government bonds may have their place, too. In recent years, banks have developed equity-linked certificates of deposit (ELCDs). These operate much like a traditional CD but with a higher potential rate of return that follows the growth of the stock market.

Annuities have also evolved in recent years. Many self-proclaimed financial advisers are little more than annuity salesmen and they've given annuities a bad rap. Years ago, annuities were often rigid and inflexible, with unacceptable options. Rules on survivorship were especially horrendous. If you died a few months after investing your money in an annuity, the insurance company kept all your money; it didn't matter if you or your beneficiaries never saw a cent. As you might expect, annuities were a hard sell and the laughingstock of the finance community.

Much has changed since the old days, though. In the late 1990s, the insurance industry realized the American public was weary of old-school annuities, and they decided to give the concept a makeover. Back in the day, an annuity worked this way: You, the hopeful soon-to-be retiree, contractually signed over a lump sum of money to an insurance company. At some point, when you wanted to make that lump sum a sustainable income source, you would "annuitize" your contract. After annuitizing the contract, you bequeathed any money that might remain in the annuity at the time of your death to the insurance company. Inheritors got squat.

Modified annuities dispensed with the need to annuitize. Instead, you could exercise the income option and whatever remained in your account after death would go to your heirs, including any appreciation. Almost overnight, annuities became the hottest "new" product. Since the annuity concept was revised, annuity sales have risen in leaps and bounds. According to one life insurance market research association, "In 2016, total fixed annuity sales hit a record-breaking $117.4 billion, 14 percent higher than 2015 levels." [76]

So, what does that mean for you? Let's be clear, annuities are not for everyone. Nor should annuities make up the bulk of your retirement portfolio, as some would contend. You shouldn't expect annuities to fill the sections of your portfolio where your objective is to achieve long-term market growth. You also shouldn't put money into an annuity if you think you may need those funds for daily living expenses now. Insurance companies expect you to let that money sit until you retire, and it's not always easy to get it back in the event of emergency. Most insurance companies will allow you to withdraw 10 percent of your balance each year without penalty *at most*. Any more than that will incur a "surrender charge." These penalties can range from 6 to 14 percent, although they normally decrease with each year of your contract until finally reaching zero. If that's not enough liquidity for your circumstances, annuities may not be for you.

Annuities can make for a productive addition to many investment plans. The best way to evaluate whether annuities fit your needs is to consult with your financial adviser.

---

[76] LIMRA. ThinkAdvisor. February 21, 2017. "Fixed Annuity Sales Hit Record $117.4 Billion in 2016."
https://www.thinkadvisor.com/2017/02/21/fixed-annuity-sales-hit-record-117-4-billion-in-20/?slreturn=20190431104326

Income Riders

Income riders are another commonly heard but often misunderstood construct. You might think of them this way: income riders are to insurance contracts what add-ons are to automobiles. These days, income riders are like the option of a radio in your car—most people just don't buy insurance plans without one. There is some variation in income rider types, but they all accomplish the same thing: You get guaranteed lifetime income and you don't have to annuitize your contract.

Many annuities make gains based on the performance of some market index (fixed index annuities, anyway). The fee for income riders on such policies—if a fee exists at all—is 1 percent or less and will be automatically deducted from those gains. When the market is down and annuity return is zero, income rider fees are taken from the account balance. That means that, even though fixed index annuities don't lose value based on market downturns, you may still see some decrease in your account balance if you own an income rider that costs additional fees.

It's worth mentioning that income rider payout is not directly calculated based on your account balance. It's based on what's called the *income account value,* which grows at a separate rate from your actual account value. The income account will normally grow from between 4 and 8 percent per year *if income is not taken.* As soon as you start drawing income, however, the income account stops growing. Naturally, then, it's wise to resist triggering an income rider for as long as possible to maximize the eventual payouts. Just to be clear, every contract is different. The aforementioned structure is a generality, but it's important to understand how many contracts are designed so that you're not caught unawares.

I ought to mention that most of the benefits outlined above are with respect to fixed index annuities (FIAs). Most annuities, however, are variable annuities—about two-thirds of all annuity offerings. Variable annuities come with many of the same benefits as FIAs, but they are an investment vehicle that does, in fact, rise and fall with the stock market. That introduces a level of volatility that may discourage some retirees. Some variable annuities also come with substantial hidden fees, as I mentioned earlier in this book. For these reasons and more, great care must be taken in deciding whether a variable annuity will make a valuable contribution to your retirement portfolio.

CHAPTER TEN

What Will Be Your Legacy?

R ay Bradbury wrote in his landmark novel *Fahrenheit 451,* "Everyone must leave something behind when he dies . . . A child or a book or a painting or a house or a wall built, or a pair of shoes made . . . something your hand touched some way, so your soul has somewhere to go when you die, and when people look at that tree or that flower you planted, you're there." In one way or another, we all leave behind a legacy. What we want our legacy to be varies from person to person. Some will leave a sizable inheritance to their children. Others leave money and assets to their favorite charities. Some want the last check they write to bounce. Whatever the case may be, it takes forethought and planning to ensure your legacy survives in the way you hope.

Of all the people in the world, you might think celebrities would understand the value of estate planning. After all, they stand to lose a lot more than the average person and can certainly afford to hire expert advisers and planners. Yet, many household names leave a financial mess in the wake of their deaths. In some cases, their heirs have lost millions of dollars in potential inheritance and sacrificed years fighting for estate custody in the court system. Following are just a few examples of financial blunders from the rich and famous.

The Celebrity: Prince. **The Mistake:** Leaving no will.

The world was shocked in April 2016 when pop icon Prince passed away. He was relatively young at fifty-seven and his lifestyle at the time didn't appear to foretell a premature death. The news became more shocking when it was revealed that Prince had left no will. Furthermore, he was not married and had no children. That left a Minnesota judge with the weighty responsibility to distribute Prince's $300 million estate.

As you might imagine, "relatives" appeared out of thin air. It seemed like half of Minnesota claimed some relation to the late music star. Besides the $300 million, Prince earned royalties on his published music, the rights to which were heavily contested. Then it was reported he had thousands of songs that had never been released. Who had the right to decide what would happen with those?

Even when Prince's rightful heirs were finally identified, it would take years before they saw a cent of inheritance, and not before taxes claimed about half the estate and lawyers another hefty chunk.[77]

The Celebrity: Marlon Brando. **The Mistake:** Making only verbal promises.

Marlon Brando was old school. His character in "The Godfather" put a lot of stock in oral contracts and the value of one's word and it seems like Mr. Brando lived by that same creed in real life. When the actor died in 2004 his estate was valued at around $100 million. That included a beautiful house, which a certain Angela Borzla had maintained for years. After Brando died, Ms. Borzla claimed the actor had promised her the house by

---

[77] Eghrari. *Forbes.* April 18, 2018. "Two Years Later, Prince's Heirs Have Still Not Received a Penny of His Estate."
https://www.forbes.com/sites/markeghrari/2018/04/18/two-years-later-princes-heirs-have-still-not-received-a-penny-of-his-estate/#512c5763ab22

way of verbal contract. Unfortunately, the written estate plan said otherwise. Borzla's claim must have had some merit, however. Her lawyers sued the estate for $2 million in punitive damages and eventually settled for $125,000—not bad, but a bit short of a $100 million mansion.[78]

The Celebrity: Michael Jackson. **The Mistake:** Failure to fund a trust.

"The King of Pop" made a better effort to support his inheritors than did his contemporary, Prince, but in the end Jackson's estate still found itself under a judge's control. You see, Michael Jackson was reportedly bankrupt at the time of his death. But that didn't mean his estate was valueless. By 2016, seven years after his death, Jackson's estate was worth $750 million. That's what Sony paid for the rights to a catalog of the artist's music. Jackson's inheritors saw little or none of that money. "But he had a trust," you might be thinking, "How can that be?" The problem was Jackson failed to *fund* his trust. On its own, a trust does little to protect one's assets. If assets are not properly titled to the trust, they still fall under the jurisdiction of the court system to settle things. That left Jackson's family in a mess, similar to the one Prince would later leave behind. As talented as he was, Michael Jackson failed in many areas of his life and within his family. This included his failure to provide a stable inheritance.[79]

The Celebrity: Heath Ledger. **The Mistake:** Omitting a child.

Heath Ledger was in a bad place at the time of his tragic suicide. He was such a skilled method actor that, when hired to play "The

---

[78] Barbara M. Pizzolato. Pizzolato Law Blog. June 30, 2016. "Estate Planning by Marlon Brando . . . Perils of Promises."
https://pizzolatolaw.com/blogestate-trust-administrationestate-planning-marlon-brando-perils-of-promises/
[79] Julie Garber. *The Balance.* January 10, 2019. "Michael Jackson's Family Trust."
https://www.thebalance.com/what-does-the-michael-jackson-family-trust-say-3505325

Joker" in the 2008 installment of the *Batman* series, Ledger wholeheartedly embraced the character's psychoses. Sadly, he was never able to eschew that persona entirely. It likely contributed to his overdose that same year.

Despite his demons, Ledger was a family man. At the time of his death, Ledger's daughter, Matilda, was two years old. Unfortunately, she was inadvertently disinherited from his will. Instead, the entirety of Mr. Ledger's $20 million estate was left to his parents and sisters. That probably wasn't the actor's intention, but he hadn't updated his will since *before* his daughter had been born. To avoid mistakes of omission, a competent legal team should *always* phrase to your will to include unnamed future children unless you stipulate otherwise.[80]

The Celebrity: Marilyn Monroe. **The Mistake:** Lack of specificity.

The beautiful Marilyn Monroe was smarter than the media often portrayed, and she did a better job of outlining her wishes than some of the other celebrities we've looked at. Still, it wasn't quite enough to spare her inheritors a measure of heartache.

When Ms. Monroe died in 1962, her estate was distributed as per her will. Some was left to her mother and to close friends. Most of her estate, however, was bequeathed to her acting coach Lee Strasberg—about 75 percent. But what would happen after Strasberg died in 1982?

Monroe probably never considered the wealth her estate would continue to accrue in the decades following her death. She

---

[80] Joanna Grossman and Mitchell Gans. FindLaw Legal Commentary. May 12, 2008. "Heath Ledger's Estate: Why Daughter Matilda, Who Was Left Nothing in Her Father's Will, Might Have a Claim to Everything."
https://supreme.findlaw.com/legal-commentary/heath-ledgers-estate-why-daughter-matilda-who-was-left-nothing-in-her-fathers-will-might-have-a-claim-to-everything.html

may have wanted that money left to members of her family or other close friends. Instead, it went exclusively to Anna Strasberg, Lee's second wife. She was a woman Marilyn barely knew. Anna assumed control of Monroe's image and rights and made millions. In 2010, the estate changed hands when it was sold for an estimated $50 million. Today, it earns about $15 million a year.

Marilyn Monroe's case isn't a wholeheartedly tragic one. Her wealth was distributed to the people she originally intended. But she may not have wanted her image under the control of a woman she didn't know. She could have avoided that eventuality by including more specific long-term stipulation for the distribution of her assets.[81]

The Woes of Probate

Probate is the process by which a court verifies and validates your will and decides how to distribute your assets. Probate can be a real headache for your loved ones and should be avoided if possible. The key is to establish not only a will, but an estate plan that oversees the distribution of assets in the event of your death. In Arizona, where my primary office operates, there are several ways to avoid the long and costly probate court proceedings.

A **living trust** operates much like a will but names a specific trustee to take primary control in the event of your death. It can thus allow beneficiaries to bypass the probate process entirely. Living trusts can oversee the transfer of just about anything you own: real estate, bank accounts, vehicles, and more. There's an important caveat. For a living trust to do its job, you must first transfer custody of your property *to yourself* as the trust's primary

---

[81] Julie Garber. *The Balance.* January 25, 2019. "A Summary of Marilyn Monroe's Last Will and Testament."
https://www.thebalance.com/marilyn-monroe-will-testament-3505094

trustee. You read that right. You sign over your rights of ownership to yourself, but through the trust. If you fail to make this critical transfer, the trust is useless. It doesn't make a whole lot of sense, but who said the legal system was designed to make sense, anyway?

Joint ownership is another way to avoid probate. If you share ownership of property and the arrangement explicitly includes "rights of survivorship," the surviving owner will immediately inherit full ownership when you die. Under joint ownership are some more specific provisions. **Joint tenancy** is common among couples (even unmarried) who acquire property together and own equal shares. When one member of the couple dies, ownership passes to the survivor. **Community property with right of ownership** is similar and unique to Arizona as a community property state. Unless married people take steps to keep their properties separate and individually owned, the state of Arizona recognizes all property acquired during the time of marriage as jointly owned. When one spouse dies, all property transfers to the survivor. This can be good or bad depending on your circumstances, and deserves careful consideration as you walk through your estate planning.

So, What Should You Do?

Tax and estate planning and the financial planning process are inextricable. I often see clients who think of the processes as separate. They hire a financial adviser to strictly manage their portfolio and a legal adviser to help them set up a will and estate plan, but the two professionals never meet. As you might imagine, that makes it hard for either to assess the big picture. That's why I chose to include an onsite legal team at my office, our sister company, Keystone Law Firm, so that every detail in a client's financial world is accounted for in their long-term planning.

Besides working as a commercial pilot, for a time I was a flight instructor. I often advised new pilots to scan the "six-pack." The six-pack is what pilots call the main instrument cluster in a traditional cockpit. It comprises six gauges, each of which is essential to a safe flying experience. There's a reason all six are tightly nestled together. While each gives distinct information, a pilot needs all six to evaluate the bigger picture and ensure normal flying conditions. Each gauge provides important insight, but the combined output of all six paints an even clearer picture.

The same is true in financial planning. Investment, retirement, tax, insurance, life, and estate planning should be integrated. Each addresses a specific area of your financial picture, but only when you put them together can you be confident your finances, now and in the future, are organized to your satisfaction.

CHAPTER ELEVEN

The Retirement Keystone

You may be aware by now that my firm is called "Keystone Wealth Partners." There's a reason for that. I'm not much of a builder, but I do love architecture. I remember years ago, probably in elementary school, when I first learned about arches and keystones.

It's easy to take arches for granted. They're such a basic architectural element these days. We see them everywhere—the Gateway Arch in St. Louis, the Arc de Triomphe in Paris, and the Victory Gate in Munich, to name a few. Besides famous monuments, arches appear in more utilitarian roles as bridges, aqueducts, and buildings.

It's hard to say who really invented the arch. There are examples of arch-like structures almost as far back as known history goes. But it was the ancient Romans who discovered the arch's immense potential after learning the fundamentals from the Etruscans. You've probably heard that all roads lead to Rome. Well, those roads would never have existed, or at least have spanned such distances, were it not for the arch.

And yet, as unappreciated as the arch is, its most important piece gets even less credit: the humble keystone. Arches stand based on the principle of compressive stress. The arch's own weight is directed in such a way to lend it strength. Pressure is directed down and out along the length of the arch and finally into the ground. What makes the arch especially impressive is it often doesn't need additional support to maintain its structure. The individual stones aren't held together with mortar. Instead, they stay in place just by the magic of physics. None of it would work, however, without the keystone.

The keystone is the central feature of an arch. It's the wedge-shaped stone that sits at the very top, against which all the other stones lean. It's the last piece installed in an arch, and it's the most important. Sure, all the other stones are necessary, but the keystone is what unites them all. It's what makes an arch *an arch*.

Can you see yet why I named my company after the keystone? Most people I meet have all the pieces of their financial life, but they don't know what to do with them to achieve the retirement they want. It's like they have all the stones of an arch except for the keystone. They're most of the way there, but without a bit of help, none of the pieces in their investment portfolio work together to accomplish their goals.

The goal in retirement is to create durable income that will last over several decades and maintain your standard of living even as living expenses inflate and earning potential diminishes. When you're still working, it's relatively easy to plan for expenses. You know exactly how much money is coming your way on a regular basis. Things get more challenging when you can't rely on a steady work income. Without a comprehensive plan, how can you be confident you'll have what you need over the next thirty years?

With pensions all but a thing of the past and Social Security under-funded, it's getting harder for retirees to evaluate their "guaranteed" income. Baby boomers are having to rely more heavily on their own investments to fund their retired lives. It can be a daunting task to organize and protect investments to sustain income for several decades.

That's where a qualified financial adviser comes in. Like a keystone, a skilled financial planner should be the piece in your retirement plan that makes everything fit together.

Can You Do It Yourself?

There are two areas in life where a do-it-yourself attitude can lead to serious trouble: your health and your wealth. Everyone has friends or family members who resist visits to the doctor. They'd rather wait until pain or sickness escalates beyond the scope of over-the-counter drugs before finally agreeing to consult a professional. In the most extreme cases, some have lost their lives because they procrastinated too long. By the time they seek a doctor's help, it may be too late.

One article published on the Cancer Research UK website says people with conditions like bowel, breast, and ovarian cancer can pretty easily survive their diseases for longer, as long as they are identified early enough. For example, "90 percent of women diagnosed with the earliest stage ovarian cancer survive their disease for at least five years compared to 5 percent for women diagnosed with the most advanced stage of the disease." The reason many people do not get treatment early enough, according to the article, is that there is a "Low awareness of cancer signs and symptoms . . . people don't realise that a symptom is important, or that they should see their doctor about it."[82]

While the ramifications of neglecting to seek financial advice may not cost us our lives, it might be flirting with financial disaster. That's why I recommend leaving financial planning to the professionals. Granted, many have taken it upon themselves to learn technical analysis, stock market trading, real estate

---

[82] Cancer Research UK. June 26, 2018. "Why is Early Diagnosis Important?" https://www.cancerresearchuk.org/about-cancer/cancer-symptoms/why-is-early-diagnosis-important

investing, and more. They may even have experienced some success in the investment world. But those people are the minority. Most who take a do-it-yourself approach find themselves losing money when their emotions get in the way, when they mistime the market, and when they throw their money at investment duds. Many people's lack of experience with the complexities of retirement is what gets them in trouble. Self-managing in the accumulation phase of life is much simpler by comparison, and it gives some retirees a false sense of competency. Retirement is a different ballgame and it can be easy for things to go wrong. By the time some DIY retirement investors finally look for a financial adviser's assistance, their situation is often like a cancer patient who's diagnosed too late: There's only so much a professional can do.

It's much better to consult with a respectable and experienced financial adviser from the get-go to ensure that your money is wisely invested, and your retirement secured.

Communication is Key

In the next chapter, I'll discuss some of the specific qualifications to look for in an adviser. But for now, I want to stress the importance of open and frank communication. For doctors to do their jobs, they need patients to be forthright and honest with them about their background, health, and symptoms. Clients must be the same with their financial advisers.

In turn, a good adviser will be open and straightforward with clients. You probably wouldn't trust a doctor who keeps his credentials secret, who doesn't listen to you, and who is vague about the treatment he prescribes. Financial professionals should be eager to hear from you, to learn about your goals and objectives, and to explain in detail any investment plan they recommend.

When you first consult with an adviser, ask who your contact will be at the office. How often will you have access to them? Who exactly will be on your team? Will one of the firm's principals be directly involved in developing your plan? How is the firm paid? Answers to these questions will give you an idea of the company's competence and their personal interest in your financial situation.

No matter what, your adviser should be an open book. If you feel a firm is withholding information about themselves or their practices, find advice elsewhere.

CHAPTER TWELVE

You Can Choose Your Own Pilot

The skies are dangerous for birds these days. Beside the threat of natural predation, a new threat has arisen in the last hundred years or so: airplanes. From the very beginning, planes have been bad news for the unsuspecting bird. In 1908, Orville Wright himself was at the helm for the first plane-bird incident, although, reportedly, he chased the bird down on purpose. (Kind of makes you wonder what sort of guy Mr. Wright was . . .)

Since then, birds have suffered more and more frequent causalities in the territory over which they once ruled sovereign. Recently, tens of thousands of birds have been struck by airplanes every year. Most of the time, as you might imagine, the birds are quickly and ignominiously killed. But sometimes the birds make a final stand. That's what happened on January 15, 2009.[83]

It's hard to imagine that birds can do anything premeditatedly; the expression "bird-brained" was coined for a reason. But if ever there seemed to be an organized stand against the metal predators

---

[83] Ed Brotak. *Aviation History.* May 2016.
https://www.historynet.com/when-birds-strike.htm

that have taken over the skies, it would have to have been the wintry day U.S. Airways flight 1549 took off from La Guardia airport in New York. Everything appeared normal before departure. Weather conditions were favorable for the brief flight headed to Charlotte Douglas Airport in North Carolina. It was a busy day, though, and air traffic control was eager to get planes off quickly while ground crews maintained a safe runway—plowing snow and clearing ice. At 3:25 p.m., the flight was cleared for departure and took off without hitch, beginning its ascent to cruising altitude.

Just after take-off, co-pilot Jeff Skiles assumed control, flying the airplane. Captain Chesley "Sully" Sullenberger sat to Skiles' left, working the radio and attending to routine tasks. As they climbed to 15,000 feet, the plane reached about 230 miles per hour. Just then, a few seconds after 3:27 p.m., a dark cloud appeared on the horizon, a row of hazy specks. Skiles saw it first. In a moment's time, the specks came into focus: a formation of Canadian Geese. Skiles barely had time to alert Captain Sullenberger before the birds descended on the aircraft. As Sully would later recall, the mob of geese seemed to fill the windscreen, cutting off visibility.

Whether the geese knew what they were doing or not, their suicide flight could hardly have done a better job of incapacitating the 150,000-pound Airbus A320. The impact was severe enough that onboard recorders captured the string of thumps as goose bodies collided with the cockpit. More struck the nose, wings, tail, and fuselage. That onslaught alone would not have crippled the massive plane, but a significant number flew directly into the engines on both sides of the plane.

The average flyer may not think birds pose a serious threat to aircraft engines, but that's only because engine designers have been careful to make allowance for interference even with entire flocks of birds. But even the largest engines are only rated to survive the ingestion of 16 *small* birds at a time—small being 3.2 ounces or less. A "small" goose weighs about seven pounds, or 112 ounces. That makes a single goose more than twice the weight of an entire test flock. U.S. Airways flight 1549 hit several geese.

In times of airplane crisis, passengers are often helpless. Most if not all on board were unqualified to address the situation. All they could hope for was a capable pilot. Fortunately, Flight 1549 was captained by one of the best.

As the cabin filled with the stench of incinerated birds, Captain Sully calmly declared, "my aircraft," and assumed control. Those who know him describe Sully as a generally calm man, and especially composed in an aircraft. His composure did not fail him as the situation became dire.

At about 3:28 p.m. Captain Sullenberger reported to the controller, "This is, uh, Cactus 1549—hit birds. We lost thrust in both engines. We're turning back toward La Guardia."

The controller in turn called the tower at La Guardia. "Tower, stop your departures," he said, "we got an emergency returning."

"Who is it?" the tower responded.

"It's 1549. He, uh . . . bird strike. He lost all engines. He lost the thrust in his engines."

There was silence over the phone as the tower officers processed their disbelief. Finally, "Cactus 1549 . . . Which engines?"

This time the controller's impatience was more obvious. "He lost thrust in *both* his engines!"

"Got it," came the curt reply.

The controller turned his attention back to Sully. La Guardia airport has two runways that intersect, allowing airplanes to land from four directions. They're not long runways. Each extends about 7,000 feet. The controller advised Captain Sullenberger to land on Runway 1-3. Sully's response was quick; he'd already decided his course of action, "We're unable. We may end up in the Hudson."

In the immediate wake of what would later be christened the "Miracle on the Hudson," some criticized Captain Sully's decision-making process. La Guardia seemed to be in range, and just about any situation is favorable to a water landing in a commercial airliner. Moreover, Teterboro Airport was also nearby and available for an emergency landing. That was the controller's next recommendation. But Sully knew neither option was possible. He knew La Guardia was about as ill-suited to a crash landing as any airport can be. On one end it is nestled into the heart of Queens. The rest abuts the busy Long Island Sound, littered with bridges, causeways, and industrial water vessels. It's the wrong place to over-shoot or under-shoot the runway. And Teterboro just wasn't realistic; it was out of reach. Later simulations would confirm that Sully's instinct had been right: A runway landing would have ended in catastrophe and the certain loss of passenger lives.

Even as the controller offered one solution after another, Captain Sully was squaring up for a river landing. It was the best chance of survival. In one final correspondence with the controller before impact Sully announced his intention again. This time he was resolute. "We're going to be in the Hudson."

The controller was flabbergasted. "I'm sorry, say again, Cactus?" he responded.

But the Captain did not repeat. Radio correspondence was at the bottom of his priorities. He had more than 150 lives to protect. His final words before touching down were to the cabin. "Brace for impact!" he announced.

As the Airbus A320 approached the calm Hudson, Sully slowed below glide speed and pulled the nose up into a flare. The fuselage struck the water's surface first and violently ruptured. Still, the Captain held tight to his controls and prevented the plane from slamming down. Within a few seconds, the vessel had crashed to a halt. The bulkhead was damaged but remained mostly intact, and no one was severely injured. Cabin crew and passengers alike were shocked when they finally looked outside and realized they had landed in water. Captain Sullenberger assisted the crew in directing passengers off the plane and into safety rafts. When everyone had disembarked, with the water level rising, Sully made two more rounds through the cabin to make sure everyone had exited. Then he boarded the final raft as the A320 sank slowly behind him.

One hundred fifty-five people could have died that day. They didn't because Captain Chesley Sullenberger was in command.[84]

An Important Decision

It's unlikely any passengers on board U.S. Airways flight 1549 knew who their pilot was when they boarded. They surely didn't know much about his qualifications and expertise. After all, every commercial pilot is competent and well-trained. But those passengers couldn't have known that their captain had been flying since he was sixteen years old, that he enlisted in the Air Force when he was eighteen, and that he'd flown commercially for several decades after his retirement from the military. Their captain was the best of the best: he had the finest training and a wealth of experience. When circumstances demanded that he adjust to a new set of variables, Chesley Sullenberger demonstrated his extraordinary ability.

The path to retirement can be likened to a flight. It's a journey, and it involves several steps to arrive safely at your destination— retirement. But you have a unique advantage over the passengers on a literal plane.

---

[84] Chesley B. Sullenberger and Jeffrey Zaslow. William Morrow Paperbacks. August 9, 2016. *Sully: My Search for What Really Matters.*

You can choose your pilot.

In this book, I've stressed that retirement does not come without its obstacles; every person's financial situation is different. There is no "one-size-fits-all" retirement process.

Imagine walking into a high-end department store to buy a pair of shoes. After browsing for a moment, you find a pair you like.

"I'd like to try these on, please," you say to a salesperson.

"Certainly," he responds, and goes to the back to fetch a pair. He returns in a moment with a pair of shoes, size nine.

"Oh, but you didn't ask my size," you say, "I need a size twelve."

"I'm terribly sorry," says the salesperson, "we only sell size nine shoes here."

That would be ridiculous, right? You can't wear a pair of shoes three sizes too small. And what kind of shoe store sells only one size, anyway? Not the kind that stays in business for very long.

The notion of a one-size-fits-all retirement plan is just as ridiculous. Yet some "advisers" stay in business with just that strategy. It's not always obvious when a financial adviser operates that way. The key to selecting a good adviser is to take your time and guarantee that his or her process fits your needs and circumstances.

First, any adviser who is not a fee-based fiduciary has the capacity to rip you off. That's not to say a non-fiduciary is always nefarious, but they aren't required *by law* to look out for your best interests. Fiduciaries, on the other hand, are held to similar standards as CPAs and attorneys. At these firms, client protection is paramount and legally enforced. Fee-based, independent, Registered Investment Adviser firms and their representatives (also known as fiduciaries) don't make money on your transactions. They don't earn commission on investment products. The only money they get is the fee you voluntarily pay if you're satisfied with services rendered. You can ensure an adviser fits this description by asking if they are a representative of a "Registered Investment Adviser." You should also confirm they are not affiliated with any broker-dealers. If an adviser works for a Registered Investment Adviser firm and has no affiliation of any kind with a broker-dealer, you're headed in the right direction. You can be confident that adviser will not push commissionable securities on behalf of his or her firm. This is critical to objective, conflict-free advice.

Second, a Registered Investment Adviser firm should be staffed by credentialed advisers. Personally, I would look for the following credentials: CERTIFIED FINANCIAL PLANNER™ (CFP®), CHARTERED FINANCIAL CONSULTANT® (ChFC), CHARTERED RETIREMENT PLANNING COUNSELOR (CRPC), or RETIREMENT INCOME CERTIFIED PROFESSIONAL (RICP®). Ideally your adviser holds a master's degree or doctorate in finance. Does that mean advisers without these qualifications aren't good at their jobs? No, not necessarily. But is it worth entrusting your money to someone without the credentials and education you would expect from an expert in personal finance? Probably not.

Third, a wealth management firm should include a Certified Public Accountant (CPA), and an estate planning attorney. Ideally this coordination is built into the firm, but at the very least, it is integrated as a network of professional relationships. At Keystone, we have a CPA and full tax practice, as well as estate planning attorneys. To me, this is particularly important because, with the image of a keystone being my mission, this gives our clients tax, legacy, and financial planning all done under one arch. A comprehensive team approach ensures all pieces of a client's financial foundation are smoothly working in concert, and they don't have to play the game of running back and forth between various professionals' offices playing financial telephone. At the very least, you want your financial professional to work with a tax planner and estate attorney in some capacity, but often I find those operating with loose professional ties might struggle to pick each other out of a lineup. Instead, be sure whomever you choose as your adviser spends time working closely with other professionals to collaborate and strategize your plan.

Wherever you are on your financial flight, whether heading into retirement or just starting to invest, you can be sure difficulties will arise along the way. You may face corrosive inflation, turbulent hidden fees, unexpected taxes, and more. You may watch as the financial atmosphere darkens around you and stock market downturns brew on the horizon. It can seem scary at times, but there's no reason to fear. A qualified financial adviser will be there to show you the way, to instill confidence in your investment portfolio, and to make sure you stay on course. Take your time choosing the adviser for you. You'll know when you've found the right one. Your adviser should develop a plan that matches your unique circumstances. Your plan should account for your hopes, dreams, and goals, and should see to it that you not only arrive safely at financial success, but that you enjoy the journey to get there. My firm's mission is to help our clients "live richly." You deserve to live your best possible life, and money— whether we like it or not—is an important part of the equation. Make sure your money enriches your life rather than adds stress to it. I wish you the best on your financial journey. As I conclude each segment of my radio show, I'll conclude this book with the same statement: "We are the wealthiest society in the history of planet earth. Let's make our money matter."

Why Did I Become an Investor Coach?

by Larry Warren, CRPC®

oney management encompasses some of the most important decisions any of us will make in our lives, and my goal has always been the same: to do the right thing for my clients and to help investors make wise decisions about their life savings. Yet, for many of the thirty years I worked as a financial adviser under the umbrella of a larger investment firm, I was unsatisfied with the service I was allowed to provide my clients.

Allow me to explain. Money is an emotional subject. Many people struggle to step back and look at their financial situation objectively. I get it. Money allows us to care for our families, to maintain our standard of living, to contribute to society. How can you remove emotion from the equation? That's where a financial adviser is supposed to step in, to help make financial decisions in an impartial, logical way. For decades, I worked for a firm that led the client to believe the adviser's job was pretty straightforward: to synthesize client objectives and compile a portfolio of investment products that matched their goals.

In reality, this process of complete adviser authority benefitted everyone but the investor. The products of the big-box parent company, which we were encouraged to promote, were designed to line the pockets of Wall Street bigwigs and keep large investment firms in the black. Minimal care was taken to ensure clients had the strongest portfolios for their needs. In my experience, there were three fundamental problems with their system, which focused on sales and product distribution rather than guidance:

1. The "adviser" was discouraged from disclosing too much information about investment products. Instead, clients got a prospectus on each recommended product, as if that would prepare them to make an informed decision. As you can imagine, more often than not, clients acquiesced to the opinion of their adviser. That was not always in their best interests.

2. There was a built-in conflict of interest. After meeting with clients and discerning some basic goals, advisers were tasked with finding appropriate products—and selling them. In many cases, what the adviser deemed "appropriate" was the product that earned him the highest commission. Time and again I'd see firms caught in this duplicitous practice and fined by the government for malpractice. One of the largest broker-dealers in the country settled a 75-million-dollar violation for favoring a mutual fund that earned the company hundreds of millions in financial kickbacks.[85] But for every firm caught acting nefariously, I bet there were five that got away with such corruption. The broker-

---

[85] Securities and Exchange Commission. December 22, 2004. "Edward Jones to Pay $75 Million to Settle Revenue Sharing Charges."
https://www.sec.gov/news/press/2004-177.htm

dealer that paid the massive fine was allowed to receive kickbacks moving forward—the "infraction" that earned them a fine in the first place—so long as the company disclosed them on a back page of their website. What kind of punishment is that? In 2018 alone, that giant firm earned over $200 million from their favorite fund companies.[86] Yet, although it is ultimately the clients' money that enables this back-scratch system, good luck finding a line item for a client getting a kickback for their contribution.

3. Investors were discouraged from understanding their adviser's role, and it had dramatic financial implications. Most investors didn't understand the difference between the suitability standard and a fiduciary standard.

A quick breakdown of the two standards the financial world uses: advisers under the suitability standard are required to recommend products suitable to a client's situation, meaning the client must be able to afford a product. That standard does not require advisers to act in their client's best interests. An adviser operating only under a suitability standard can sell things that are in their own best interest as long as what they are selling isn't ridiculous. Many advisers in the traditional broker space I worked in were only required to operate under the vague suitability standard, meaning they could legally put their profit as a higher standard than their people.

For these reasons and more, I eventually couldn't stand to work as a traditional broker anymore. I converted my practice to an independent model based on coaching, and eventually joined my son-in-law's firm at Keystone Wealth Partners. To illustrate how the coaching model works, imagine a literal sports team. The coach may have been the greatest to ever play the game, but in his

---

[86] Edward Jones. 2019. "Revenue Sharing Disclosure."
https://www.edwardjones.com/images/revenue-sharing-disclosure.pdf

role as a coach, it doesn't matter. His job is to develop his players' skills, prepare a game plan, and encourage the athletes to perform well. He only wins when his team wins.

This format can also apply to the investment world, and it holds advisers accountable to their clients. Both parties are working toward the same goal and benefit from mutual success. As an investor coach, my role is threefold. First, I want to develop my investor team member skills to equip my clients for success in the financial world. Second, I aim to structure a financial plan that gives investors the best chance of financial success in the long term. Third, I hold my clients accountable to their financial plans. I've seen tremendous success since implementing this style of investment advice in 2013. Many traditional advisers want the best for their clients, but they're stifled and limited by the confines of large brokerage firms' bottom lines and corrupt investment agencies' expectations.

I know this because I used to be one of them. I became a broker in 1987 with a desire to help people build their futures. Over the years, it became increasingly difficult to meet that goal with the stresses and influence of greedy firms that dominate the industry. Before shifting my focus and gaining independence from the big players, my health was on a sharp decline. My stress came from being restricted to explaining features and benefits of commission-based products rather than having the freedom to collaborate with each client and do only what was in their best interests.

As an independent investor coach, not only are my clients more confident in the quality of their financial plans, but I have a strong belief that I am truly helping people live their best possible lives. At Keystone Wealth Partners, acting with tax professionals and estate planners to collaborate on all the parts of a financial strategy means knowing the whole picture and custom-tailoring that to each person, not just making transactional sales. After so many decades in this industry, I am finally excited about what I can do for clients, and I look forward to helping investors for many years yet to come!

Larry W. Warren

Proudly, an Investor Coach

Larry W. Warren, CRPC® is a Keystone Wealth Partners Financial Adviser at the North Dakota Office. A "reformed" broker after twenty-five years, he has focused on holistic financial coaching since 2013. Prior to entering the financial profession, he was a corporate pilot and has over 5,000 flight hours. Larry is married to his high school sweetheart, has two children, is a devoted grandfather, and is proud to be John Hagensen's father-in-law.

About the Author

Whether it comes to being a pilot, ensuring a safe flight requires the unique ability to decisively adapt as conditions emerge. It is this kind of precision and attention to detail that make John Hagensen not only an exceptional pilot, but also led him to build one of Arizona's most respected financial planning firms.[87]

John is the Founder and Managing Director of Keystone Wealth Partners. His vision for starting KWP was to deliver financial planning strategies free from Wall Street's embedded conflicts of interest. Today, clients benefit from these strategies targeted to meet their unique needs.

As a thought leader in the industry, John is driven by his desire to find new and interesting ways to educate investors. Having the heart of a teacher, his approach is educational and consultative. He is passionate about coaching his clients to remain disciplined to a long-term, academically sound strategy and executes this through monthly group coaching sessions. His intention to inform Main Street investors is also demonstrated through his weekly radio show, *Myth Busting with Keystone Wealth Partners*, as well as through

---

[87] Ranking Arizona ranked Keystone Wealth Partners one of the Top 10 Independent Financial Planning Firms in the state of Arizona in 2016.

his weekly podcast, *Rethink Your Money*. John is a sought-after public speaker and has educated thousands nearing retirement. In addition, John is an author of multiple books. His first book, *Unleash Your Investments*, hit shelves in the summer of 2017 and this, his second book, *The Retirement Flight Plan*, landed in 2020.

John has a Master of Science in Financial Services from the Institute of Business & Finance, a Strategic Decision and Risk Management Professional Certification from Stanford University and a Behavioral Finance Professional Certificate from Duke University. John holds the credentials of Certified Funds Specialist (CFS), Certified Annuity Specialist (CAS), Certified Estate & Trust Specialist (CES), Certified Tax Specialist (CTS) and Certified Income Specialist (CIS). John holds a designation from the National Social Security Association (NSSA) as well. He completed his Bachelor of Science degree at Corban University.

John is a native of Washington state and currently resides in Gilbert with his wife, Brittany, and their six children. He has many passions, but none more than adoption and social justice. After four trips to Ethiopia while adopting two of their children, sustainable, clean-water projects in Africa became a primary focus for John and his wife. As a result, Keystone donates a portion of upfront engagement fees to Charity: Water, and has donated more than $100,000 to Ethiopian villages so far. John leads a community Bible study and believes his faith is the central anchor to every component of his life and business.

He also loves all things sports, but more than sports or business, his greatest joy lies in his family. He is an avid reader and will knock out thirty nonfiction books in a typical year. As a Seattle native, he drinks way too much coffee, and his future goals include learning to speak Spanish fluently, becoming a capable pianist and continuing to run a marathon every year or two.

Contact Us

If the approach we outlined in this book to protecting and growing your wealth on a hyper-personal level resonated with you, please give us a call or email. We'd love to get to know you and see if we're a fit.

Keystone Wealth Partners
CONTACT US
Arizona: 480-782-1034
North Dakota: 701-222-3268
info@keystonewealthpartners.com

Made in the USA
Columbia, SC
17 February 2022

56000512R00105